S0-BFD-161

Quick Reference

by Stuart J. Stuple

IDG BOOKS

IDG Books Worldwide, Inc.
An International Data Group Company

San Mateo, California ♦ Indianapolis, Indiana ♦ Boston, Massachusetts

Quattro Pro 6 For Windows For Dummies Quick Reference

Published by
IDG Books Worldwide, Inc.
An International Data Group Company
155 Bovet Road, Suite 310
San Mateo, CA 94402

Library of Congress Catalog Card No.: 94-78906

ISBN: 1-56884-172-8

Printed in the United States of America

10 9 8 7 6 5 4 3 2 1

1D/RU/RQ/ZU

Distributed in the United States by IDG Books Worldwide, Inc.

Distributed in Canada by Macmillan of Canada, a Division of Canada Publishing Corporation; by Computer and Technical Books in Miami, Florida, for South America and the Caribbean; by Longman Singapore in Singapore, Malaysia, Thailand, and Korea; by Toppan Co. Ltd. in Japan; by Asia Computerworld in Hong Kong; by Woodslane Pty. Ltd. in Australia and New Zealand; and by Transworld Publishers Ltd. in the U.K. and Europe.

For general information on IDG Books in the U.S., including information on discounts and premiums, contact IDG Books 800-434-3422 or 415-312-0650.

For information on where to purchase IDG Books outside the U.S., contact Christina Turner at 415-312-0633.

For information on translations, contact Marc Jeffrey Mikulich, Foreign Rights Manager, at IDG Books Worldwide; FAX number 415-286-2747.

For sales inquiries and special prices for bulk quantities, write to the address above or call IDG Books Worldwide at 415-312-0650.

For information on using IDG Books in the classroom, or for ordering examination copies, contact Jim Kelly at 800-434-2086.

About the Author

Stuart Stuple has worked with computers since before personal computing was a reality. He got his start on a series of DEC machines running Unix, but now leads a very balanced existence — his desk has both a Macintosh and a Windows machine. In addition to work for other publishers, he is the author of the *Access 2 For Dummies Quick Reference* (by IDG Books) and several forthcoming quick references as well as having worked in various capacities on over a dozen other IDG titles. He has a Masters degree in Counseling Psychology and has been a member of the faculty at community colleges in both California and Washington. He currently works as a freelance editor and author, mostly so that he can play with new software.

ABOUT IDG BOOKS WORLDWIDE

WINNER
Eighth Annual Computer Press Awards 1992

WINNER
Ninth Annual Computer Press Awards 1993

Welcome to the world of IDG Books Worldwide.

IDG Books Worldwide, Inc., is a subsidiary of International Data Group, the world's largest publisher of business and computer-related information and the leading global provider of information services on information technology. IDG was founded more than 25 years ago and now employs more than 5,700 people worldwide. IDG publishes more than 200 computer publications in 63 countries (see listing below). Forty million people read one or more IDG publications each month.

Launched in 1990, IDG Books is today the fastest-growing publisher of computer and business books in the United States. We are proud to have received 3 awards from the Computer Press Association in recognition of editorial excellence, and our best-selling *...For Dummies* series has tens of millions of copies in print with translations in more than 20 languages. IDG Books, through a recent joint venture with IDG's Hi-Tech Beijing, became the first U.S. publisher to publish a computer book in the People's Republic of China. In record time, IDG Books has become the first choice for millions of readers around the world who want to learn how to better manage their businesses.

Our mission is simple: Every IDG book is designed to bring extra value and skill-building instructions to the reader. Our books are written by experts who understand and care about our readers. The knowledge base of our editorial staff comes from years of experience in publishing, education, and journalism — experience which we use to produce books for the '90s. In short, we care about books, so we attract the best people. We devote special attention to details such as audience, interior design, use of icons, and illustrations. And because we use an efficient process of authoring, editing, and desktop publishing our books electronically, we can spend more time ensuring superior content and spend less time on the technicalities of making books.

You can count on our commitment to deliver high-quality books at competitive prices on topics customers want to read about. At IDG, we value quality, and we have been delivering quality for more than 25 years. You'll find no better book on a subject than an IDG book.

John J. Kilcullen

John Kilcullen
President and CEO
IDG Books Worldwide, Inc.

IDG Books Worldwide, Inc., is a subsidiary of International Data Group. The officers are Patrick J. McGovern, Founder and Board Chairman; Walter Boyd, President. International Data Group's publications include: **ARGENTINA'S** Computerworld Argentina, Infoworld Argentina; **AUSTRALIA'S** Computerworld Australia, Australian PC World, Australian Macworld, Network World, Mobile Business Australia, Reseller, IDG Sources; **AUSTRIA'S** Computerwelt Oesterreich, PC Test; **BRAZIL'S** Computerworld, Gamepro, Game Power, Mundo IBM, Mundo Unix, PC World, Super Game; **BELGIUM'S** Data News (CW) **BULGARIA'S** Computerworld Bulgaria, Ediworld, PC & Mac World Bulgaria, Network World Bulgaria; **CANADA'S** CIO Canada, Computerworld Canada, Graduate Computerworld, InfoCanada, Network World Canada; **CHILE'S** Computerworld Chile, Informatica; **COLOMBIA'S** Computerworld Colombia, PC World; **CZECH REPUBLIC'S** Computerworld, Elektronika, PC World; **DENMARK'S** Communications World, Computerworld Danmark, Macintosh Produktkatalog, Macworld Danmark, PC World Danmark, PC World Produktguide, Tech World, Windows World; **ECUADOR'S** PC World Ecuador; **EGYPT'S** Computerworld (CW) Middle East, PC World Middle East; **FINLAND'S** MikroPC, Tietoviikko, Tietoverkko; **FRANCE'S** Distributique, GOLDEN MAC, InfoPC, Languages & Systems, Le Guide du Monde Informatique, Le Monde Informatique, Telecoms & Reseaux; **GERMANY'S** Computerwoche, Computerwoche Focus, Computerwoche Extra, Computerwoche Karriere, Information Management, Macwelt, Netzwelt, PC Welt, PC Woche, Publish, Unit; **GREECE'S** Infoworld, PC Games; **HUNGARY'S** Computerworld SZT, PC World; **HONG KONG'S** Computerworld Hong Kong, PC World Hong Kong; **INDIA'S** Computers & Communications; **IRELAND'S** ComputerScope; **ISRAEL'S** Computerworld Israel, PC World Israel; **ITALY'S** Computerworld Italia, Lotus Magazine, Macworld Italia, Networking Italia, PC Shopping, PC World Italia; **JAPAN'S** Computerworld Today, Information Systems World, Macworld Japan, Nikkei Personal Computing, SunWorld Japan, Windows World; **KENYA'S** East African Computer News; **KOREA'S** Computerworld Korea, Macworld Korea, PC World Korea; **MEXICO'S** Compu Edicion, Compu Manufactura, Computacion/Punto de Venta, Computerworld Mexico, MacWorld, Mundo Unix, PC World, Windows; **THE NETHERLANDS'** Computer! Totaal, Computable (CW), LAN Magazine, MacWorld, Totaal "Windows"; **NEW ZEALAND'S** Computer Listings, Computerworld New Zealand, New Zealand PC World, Network World; **NIGERIA'S** PC World Africa; **NORWAY'S** Computerworld Norge, C/World, Lotusworld Norge, Macworld Norge, Networld, PC World Ekspress, PC World Norge, PC World's Produktguide, Publish& Multimedia World, Student Data, Unix World, Windowsworld; IDG Direct Response; **PAKISTAN'S** PC World Pakistan; **PANAMA'S** PC World Panama; **PERU'S** Computerworld Peru, PC World; **PEOPLE'S REPUBLIC OF CHINA'S** China Computerworld, China Infoworld, Electronics Today/Multimedia World, Electronics International, Electronic Product World, China Network World, PC and Communications Magazine, PC World China, Software World Magazine, Telecom Product World; IDG HIGH TECH BEIJING'S New Product World; IDG SHENZHEN'S Computer News Digest; **PHILIPPINES'** Computerworld Philippines, PC Digest (PCW); **POLAND'S** Computerworld Poland, PC World/Komputer; **PORTUGAL'S** Cerebro/PC World, Correio Informatico/Computerworld, Informatica & Comunicacoes Catalogo, MacIn, Nacional de Produtos; **ROMANIA'S** Computerworld, PC World; **RUSSIA'S** Computerworld-Moscow, Mir - PC, Sety; **SINGAPORE'S** Computerworld Southeast Asia, PC World Singapore; **SLOVENIA'S** Monitor Magazine; **SOUTH AFRICA'S** Computer Mail (CIO),Computing S.A.,Network World S.A., Software World; **SPAIN'S** Advanced Systems, Amiga World, Computerworld Espana, Communicaciones World, Macworld Espana, NeXTWORLD, Super Juegos Magazine (GamePro), PC World Espana, Publish; **SWEDEN'S** Attack, ComputerSweden, Corporate Computing, Natverk & Kommunikation, Macworld, Mikrodatorn, PC World, Publishing & Design (CAP), Datalngenjoren, Maxi Data,Windows World; **SWITZERLAND'S** Computerworld Schweiz, Macworld Schweiz, PC Tip; **TAIWAN'S** Computerworld Taiwan, PC World Taiwan; **THAILAND'S** Thai Computerworld; **TURKEY'S** Computerworld Monitor, Macworld Turkiye, PC World Turkiye; **UKRAINE'S** Computerworld; **UNITED KINGDOM'S** Computing /Computerworld, Connexion/ Network World, Lotus Magazine, Macworld, Open Computing/Sunworld; **UNITED STATES'** Advanced Systems, AmigaWorld, Cable in the Classroom, CD Review, CIO, Computerworld, Digital Video, DOS Resource Guide, Electronic Entertainment Magazine, Federal Computer Week, Federal Integrator, GamePro, IDG Books, Infoworld, Infoworld Direct, Laser Event, Macworld, Multimedia World, Network World, PC Letter, PC World, PlayRight, Power PC World, Publish, SWATPro, Video Event; **VENEZUELA'S** Computerworld Venezuela, PC World; **VIETNAM'S** PC World Vietnam

Acknowledgments

The people involved in this book all deserve a special thanks. The creation of this book took place along with a move from one half of the state to the other. I'm using this opportunity to thank the people involved with both projects. As always, thanks to Bjoern — this time for being my wrists as well as support. My thanks and my love to my mother who showed up and wrapped all of my life in newspaper so that it could be packed in small boxes and trucked along. We didn't break a thing. I also couldn't have done it without the chance to let off steam. Therefore, thanks to both Devra and Merry — strange spellers, but good friends. Finally, a thanks to all of the friends at both ends of the move who helped — especially Kenny and Drew.

Holding down the fort on the book side, the key players were my project editors: Erik Dafforn who let me keep my sanity during the move and Laurie Smith who had to deal with me after I lost it and started writing. Thanks to Janna Custer and Megg Bonar for giving me the opportunity to live through this once again and especially to Megg for handling the details and putting up with my complaining. In a similar vein, I want to thank Mary Bednarek who always seems to know when I need a bit of E-mail to brighten my day.

Thanks also to both Sandy Blackthorn and Diane Steele, Senior Editors, who were able to step in and help get me back on track. I appreciate it and look forward to it never having to happen again. The copy editors, Barb Potter and Kathy Simpson, deserve both my thanks and a long vacation — you translated as fast as I can write. Thanks again to Michael Partington for his technical edit — maybe next time I'll try real science fiction. Of course, the book would have looked awfully silly the way I turned it in, so thanks to the production team, especially Kathie Schnorr who made it look good on paper. Finally, thanks to the indexer, Nancy Anderman Guenther, and the proofreader, Kathleen Prata — if you can find anything it's because of their work.

(The publisher would like to thank Patrick J. McGovern, without whom this book would not have been possible.)

Credits

Publisher
David Solomon

Managing Editor
Mary Bednarek

Acquisitions Editor
Megg Bonar

Production Director
Beth Jenkins

Senior Editors
Tracy L. Barr
Sandra Blackthorn
Diane Graves Steele

**Associate
Production Coordinator**
Valery Bourke

Editorial Assistants
Suki Gear
Tammy Castleman

Project Editors
Laurie Smith
Erik Dafforn

Editors
Barb Potter
Kathy Simpson

Technical Reviewer
Michael J. Partington

**Pre-Press
Coordinator**
Steve Peake

Production Staff
Patricia R. Reynolds
Kathie Schnorr
Gina Scott

Proofreader
Kathleen Prata

Indexer
Nancy Anderman Guenther

Contents at a Glance

Introduction

You can use the Quattro Pro For Dummies Quick Reference a number of ways. If you want to learn more about a particular command, just look it up in the main part of the book, the Command Reference. Most commands are listed by the name of the menu that they are on followed, by the command name. So you'd find the Print command under File⇨Print. Quattro Pro, however has a variety of commands that don't appear on a menu. Most of these have to do with setting the *properties* for a part of your notebook. (A property is a setting such as the color of an object or the font used in a cell.)

Because these commands aren't on a menu we had to be a little bit creative about where we put them. They appear under the name of the dialog box that they are on. So the non-menu command to set the font for a cell appears under Active Block⇨Font. If you're working on your computer and you've made it to the dialog box, you'll be able to know immediately where to look. If you know what it is you're trying to do, but not what command to use, look in the Index which will give you the page number.

The back of the book has a special section, "A Toolbar Tour," that shows you each of the Quattro Pro SpeedBars (aka toolbars) and the buttons on each. There's a quick description of each button and where to find it in the Command Reference.

For the "quick" in Quick Reference, each command lists any available shortcuts. Some of the shortcuts use the mouse, and others use the keyboard. It's the truly fortunate command which has both. The "reference" part is covered by the many tips and notes you'll find for each command.

I hope all these features combine to make your use of Quattro Pro a little bit easier and a little bit faster.

What Do These Pesky Icons Mean?

Oh, one more thing. This book is filled with funny little pictures designed to make comprehension a little easier. These pictures are called icons. The following list tells you what they signify.

 This icon flags commands that are recommended for the average Quattro Pro user.

 This icon points out commands that are not recommended for the average Quattro Pro user.

 This icon designates the kind of command that an average Quattro Pro user may not want to use, but learning this command may come in handy.

 This icon flags commands that you can safely use.

 This icon flags commands that are usually safe, but if you're not careful, you may run into trouble.

 This icon designates commands that pose some danger to your data if you don't use them correctly, so be careful. You may be better off having someone else use these commands for you.

 This icon points out commands that you should never use unless you're some kind of programmer or technical guru.

Quattro Pro's a bit unusual in that some commands can only be selected from the menu that pops up when you click the right mouse button. This icon identifies those commands as well as some where this is a useful shortcut.

 This icon warns of problem areas and potentially dangerous situations.

 This icon flags helpful information that will make life with Quattro Pro easier.

 This icon indicates a cross reference to another entry or section within this Quick Reference.

 This icon flags cross references to material in IDG's *Quattro Pro 6 For Windows For Dummies* book.

Part 1

Command Reference

Active Block dialog box

Many of Quattro Pro's commands are not found on the menus, but rather on dialog boxes that are gotten to either by using the right mouse button or the Property menu on the far right of the Property Band. The Active Block commands are one example of this type of dialog box. You won't find an Active Block choice on any of the menus. There are two ways to get to the Active Block dialog box. The one I prefer is to point to a cell or block of cells on your notebook page, click the right mouse button and select Block Properties from the pop-up menu. The other is to select a cell or block of cells, open the Property menu at the far right end of the Property Band (you can use Alt, P) and select Current Object.

When you are looking at the dialog box, you'll notice a list of choices along the left side. To select among the various options on the dialog box, click on the command you want to work with. For example, to use the dialog box to change the width of a column, you would position your cursor over the words "Column Width" and click once with the left button. The rest of the dialog box changes to the controls for that command. Sorry it's so confusing, but I didn't write the program — just the Quick Reference.

Active Block⇨Alignment

Controls the position of the information in the cells or group of cells (a *block*). You can put the contents of the cells to the far left or the far right, or you can center the contents within each cell or across the entire group of selected cells. Most often, Quattro Pro uses the General alignment, which puts values to the far right and labels to the far left.

For mouse maniacs

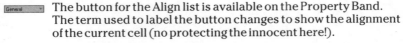 The button for the Align list is available on the Property Band. The term used to label the button changes to show the alignment of the current cell (no protecting the innocent here!).

The Vertical Alignment: Bottom button is available on the Format SpeedBar. Click on the button to make the contents of the cell (or cells) sink to the bottom of the cell.

Clicking on the Vertical Alignment: Center button (available only on the Format SpeedBar) causes the contents of the cell (or cells) to float in the middle — centered between the top and bottom of the cell.

This is the Helium button (would you believe the Vertical Align: Top button?) on the Format SpeedBar. If you click on the button, the contents of the cell (or cells) floats right up to the top of the cell.

The Word Wrap button, available only on the Format SpeedBar, keeps the text within the cell by forcing new lines between words. Normally, text just escapes to the right of the cell and hangs out with the neighbors.

The Orientation button on the Format SpeedBar changes the orientation of the text. In some cases, this change can take years of therapy, but with Quattro Pro, a single click of this button changes the way the text is displayed within the cell from reading left to right to reading up and down.

Just the facts

To change the left-to-right position of text within a cell (the *horizontal alignment*), you simply select the cells that you want to change and then select the alignment you want from the Align list on the Property Band. The Align list is the fourth button from the left. The first option is General, which puts values to the right and labels to the left. The next three options — Left, Center, and Right — align the text within the cell and ignore whether the text is a label or a value. The final option, Center across block, centers the text across any empty cells so that it appears in the middle of the block. Any blank cells to the right of the one that contains text are used, but the text actually remains in the left-most cell. It looks like it goes across all of the cells, but if you need to edit it, you'll find the text is stored in the left cell only.

Another feature that is controlled by Active Block ⇨ Alignment, but is easier to use as a button, is Word Wrap. The Word Wrap feature controls what happens when there is too much text in a label to fit into a single cell. If Word Wrap is not active (the SpeedBar button appears raised) and the cell to the right is empty, the "extra" text appears in the second cell. In other words, the label in the first cell just continues on into the empty cell or cells to the right. If there is text in the cell to the right, the text in the first cell is just cut off. If Word Wrap is active (the SpeedBar button appears pressed), the label breaks into multiple lines within the cell.

The easiest way to use Word Wrap is to display the Format SpeedBar and use the Word Wrap button. The other approach is to open the Active Block dialog box, described in the "More stuff" section. If you're working with the Active Block dialog box, the feature is controlled by the Wrap Text checkbox. With either method, you first need to select the cells you want to change.

To change the up-and-down position of the text in the cells (the *vertical alignment*), you can use either the Format SpeedBar or the Active Block dialog box. With the Format SpeedBar displayed, simply select the blocks you want to work with and then click on the appropriate vertical alignment button. For you to see a change in vertical alignment, the row height needs to be taller than the text contained within the cell. To change the row height, choose Active Block⇨Row Height.

The final option for Alignment in the Active Block dialog box (and another button on the Format SpeedBar) is the Orientation button. You can use this button to change the orientation of the text from left-to-right to top-to-bottom. The top-to-bottom orientation can be very useful for labels along the left side of your notebook page.

More stuff

There are times when you will want to enter an alignment as part of the text you are putting into a cell, such as when you are entering numbers as labels, and you want to avoid any confusion. To have the contents of the cell align to the left side, put a single quotation mark (') as the first character. To center the information, put a caret (^) as the first character (located above the 6 across the top of the keyboard). To force the contents to the right edge of the cell, put a double quotation mark (") as the first character. These options are available in the Active Block dialog box, but there's one more that you can only get by starting the label with a special character. To have the text repeat until it fills up the entire cell, start with a backslash (\) as the first character (back in the old days, that was how we used to draw lines).

If a value or the results of a formula are too wide to fit within the cell, Quattro Pro first tries to display the number in scientific notation (such as 1.3 E+09). If the cell has a numeric format (such as currency or commas) and the value is too wide, Quattro Pro displays a series of asterisks.

You can get to these commands by selecting the cells, clicking the right mouse button (while the cursor is still over the selected cells), choosing Block Properties from the pop-up menu (to open the Active Block dialog box), and then clicking on Alignment.

Of course, if you just want to change the horizontal alignment, simply use the Align list on the Property Band or, if you want to make a lot of formatting changes, select the Format SpeedBar and use its buttons. To display the Format SpeedBar, select Format from the Toolbars list (second from the right on the Property Band).

To find out how to line things up neatly, see Chapter 5 in *Quattro Pro 6 For Windows For Dummies*. To find out how to use all the formatting commands, see Chapter 12.

You can control the width of the cell (which affects the position of the aligned text) with Active Block ⇨ Column Width. After you've aligned the material, you may want to change the way it looks with Active Block ⇨ Font, or you may want to put borders around the cell with Active Block ⇨ Line Drawing.

Active Block ⇨ Column Width

Changes how wide the cell is. If you make your columns narrower, you can fit more information on the page. Of course, if your data is a bit on the heavy side, you need to make your columns wider so that the information fits in the columns well.

For mouse maniacs

To get the column-width pointer, simply put the cursor at the top of the columns, where the letters are, on the line marking the border between the columns. You can then hold down the mouse button and drag to change the column width.

Click on the Size to Fit button (on the General SpeedBar) to automatically adjust the size of the selected column(s) to the width of the largest value or label in the column.

Just the facts

The easiest way to change the column width is to move the cursor over the line between the column letters. After the cursor changes to the column-width pointer (a vertical line with arrows out each side), you can hold down the mouse button and drag the column border to a new width. The only disadvantage of this method is that you don't have any way of precisely measuring what size you make the new column. To make an accurate measurement, you need to use the Active Block dialog box.

The mouse method (and my preferred method) to get to the Active Block dialog box is to first select the cell(s) that you want to change. Click the right mouse button while the cursor is over the selected cells and then select the Block Properties option with the left mouse button.

The other way to get to the Active Block dialog box is to select your cell(s), select the Property menu on the far right of Property Band (either by clicking on it or by using Alt+P), and then select Current Object. Either method gives you the same dialog box. If you select Column Width from the list on the left of the dialog box, you'll see the following dialog box.

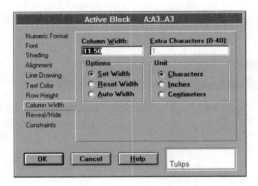

To set the width of a column, first decide what measurement units you want to use. (In general, the units don't matter much unless you want to use the Auto Width feature.) Enter a value in the Column Width box. If you're using Characters as your units, you can also enter an optional value in the Extra Character box. To set the column width, make sure to choose the Set Width option and then click on OK.

If you choose the Reset Width option, the value in the Column Width box disappears, and you will be using whatever value is set for the notebook's default column width.

You can use Auto Width to adjust the column to the width of the widest label or value plus the value that you enter in the Extra Character box. You can specify extra characters only if you are using Characters as your measurement unit.

More stuff

The problem with measuring in terms of characters is that the Characters measurement doesn't have anything to do with how many characters you can fit into the cell. Once upon a time, people used printers that were able to print only letters of the same width (so that an *I* and a *W* both used the same amount of space). Therefore, a cell with a width of nine characters could hold exactly nine characters. Today, everyone uses fancy characters that allow you to put several more *I*s into a cell than *W*s, so you can have a different number of characters in each cell. The thing you can still count on, however, is that two columns that are set as nine characters wide are the same width. (By the way, according to Quattro Pro, there are between 14 and 15 characters in an inch.)

 For an example of changing cell widths, see Chapter 4 in *Quattro Pro 6 For Windows For Dummies*. You can also find out about adjusting column widths in Chapter 10.

 You can change the height of a row by using Active Block ⇨ Row Height. You can determine the position of the text within the cell by using Active Block ⇨ Alignment. Use Active Page ⇨ Default Width to set the width of the standard column. And you can hide a column entirely by using Active Block ⇨ Reveal/Hide.

Active Block ⇨ Constraints

Enables you to require that the selected cells contain only labels or only dates. If you type a number into a cell marked as <u>L</u>abel Only, it is treated as text. A cell that has been set for <u>D</u>ates Only accepts only values in proper Quattro Pro date formats (such as Sept. 14, 1995 or 9/14/95). You also need to use this command to make cells available for data entry when you have protected the page by using Active Page ⇨ Protection. These features are most useful when you are designing a notebook page to be filled in by someone else.

Just the facts

 The mouse method (and my preferred method) to use this command in the Active Block dialog box is to select the cell(s) that you want to change, click the right mouse button while the cursor is over the selected cells, and then select (with the left mouse button) the Block Properties choice from the pop-up menu.

The other way to use this command is to select your cell(s), select the <u>P</u>roperty menu on the far right of the Property Band (either by clicking on it or by using Alt+P), and then select Current Object. Either method gives you the same dialog box. You then need to select Constraints from the list on the left of the dialog box.

There are two sections in the Constraints area of the Active Block dialog box: Cell Protection and Data Input Constraints. The Cell Protection section has two radio buttons — only one can be selected at a time — that can be used only when you have turned on Active Page⇨Protection. Cells that are marked as Unprotect can still be modified even when Page Protection is turned on. The Protect option is set by default.

The other section is Data Input Constraints. The General options means that you can put any old thing into the cell. The Labels Only option means no values. This option is convenient if you have a bunch of numbers that you want Quattro Pro to use as labels rather than values. Simply mark the cells as Labels Only before you begin entering the numbers. The final option, Dates Only, requires you to enter a value in a date format recognized by Quattro Pro. This option is useful for forcing people to do things the way you want.

More stuff

You use the constraints primarily with the Tools⇨Numeric Tools⇨Optimizer command. To protect cells from input, you need to use Active Page⇨Protection. When a page is protected, you can use Block⇨Restrict Input to further control the input of values in an unprotected block.

Active Block ⇨ Font

Controls the way the characters that you use will look. You can change the typeface or *font* (the actual shape of the characters), the size, and the options or *style* of character (bold, italic, and so on). Most of these features are also available from the Property Band or the SpeedBar.

For mouse maniacs

b　The Bold button is available on both the Main and Format SpeedBars. Click on the button, and the text in the selected cell(s) changes from bold to not bold or vice versa.

i　The Italic button (also on both the Main and Format SpeedBars) changes the text in the selected cell(s) from italic to not italic or vice versa.

u　The Underline button is available only on the Format SpeedBar. The button controls whether the text within the cell is underlined. Be aware that underlining text is different than putting a border at the bottom of the cell.

These arrows on the Format SpeedBar are used to increase (the up arrow) or decrease (the down arrow) the size of the text in the selected cell(s).

The first list, the Font list, on the Property Band controls what font is used in the selected cell(s). The button for the list is labeled with the name of the font used in the current cell.

The second list, the Font Size list, on the Property Band controls the size of the font used in the selected cell(s). The button for this list shows the font size for the current cell.

Just the facts

If you want to change only the font or the font size, simply select the blocks containing the text to be changed and then select the appropriate list. The Font list is the first list on the Property Band and includes all the fonts installed within Windows on your system. The second list is the Font Size list and changes based upon which font you have selected. To obtain a font size that is not on the list, you need to open the Active Block dialog box.

You can use the Bold and Italic buttons that appear on both the Main and Format SpeedBars to change text to either of these styles. You just select the cells you want to change and then click on the appropriate button. If a cell is already formatted and you want to remove the bold or italic formatting, simply select the cell and click on the button. Removing formatting causes the button to change from looking as though it were pressed to looking as though it were raised.

To apply underlining, you can either select the Format SpeedBar or open the Active Block dialog box. Using the SpeedBar is more efficient because you can see your changes as you make them. To open the Format SpeedBar, click on the Toolbar list on the Property Band (the next to the last list) and select Format.

Strikeout is the only font formatting that is available only via the Active Block dialog box. Strikeout is generally used to mark text that is no longer current and is to be deleted. While strikeout is often used to mark revisions in word processing, it's not used very often in spreadsheets; so it's no wonder the command is hard to get to.

More stuff

You can get to this command by selecting the cells, clicking the right mouse button (while the cursor is still over the selected cells), choosing Block Properties from the pop-up menu (to open the Active Block dialog box), and then clicking on Font. Of course, if you want to change only the font, it's a lot easier to use the lists on the Property Band and the buttons on the SpeedBar.

You really never need to use the Underline style. The contents of your cells will look much better if you use the Active Block⇨Line Drawing command to put a border on the bottom of the cell. Isn't it convenient that Line Drawing is the next command in this Quick Reference.

To find out how to use the formatting commands, see Chapter 12 in *Quattro Pro 6 For Windows For Dummies*.

You can store a font style by using Notebook⇨Define Style. To change the color of your letters, use Active Block⇨Text Color. To increase the size of the characters displayed without changing their size when printed, change the magnification by using Active Notebook⇨Zoom Factor or Active Page⇨Zoom Factor.

Active Block⇨Line Drawing

Puts borders around the cell(s) that you are working with. Of course, if the borders are already there, you can use this command to remove them. You get to control which sides of the cell(s) get borders, the type of line used, and the color of the line.

For mouse maniacs

If the Format SpeedBar is open, you can jump directly to the Line Drawing options by clicking on this button.

The fifth button on the Property Band (counting from the left) is called Underline, but it really controls whether there is a border on the bottom of the cell.

Just the facts

You can get to this command by selecting the cells, clicking the right mouse button (while the cursor is still over the selected cells), choosing Block Properties from the pop-up menu (to open the Active Block dialog box), and the clicking on the Line Drawing option in the list on the left. Of course, it's a lot easier to select the Format SpeedBar and click on the Line Draw button. Whichever method you use displays the following Line Drawing dialog box.

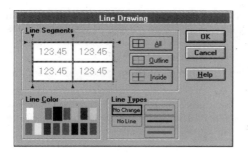

There are three sections in the Line Drawing dialog box: Line Segments, Line Types, and Line Color. The most important section is Line Segments. The grid of four boxes (each containing 123.45) represents the selected block. The outside lines represent the edges of the block, and the two inside lines represent the lines between the cells within the block. If a line in the grid has arrows at both ends, it is part of the selection, and any changes made in the dialog box will affect that border. In the figure of the Line Drawing dialog box, the top and left edges of the block as well as the vertical line between the cells are selected. You can add lines by using the buttons on the right labeled All, Outline and Inside or by holding down Shift and clicking on a line. (You can also hold down Shift and click on a line to remove it from the selection.)

After you decide which lines to change, you can use the options in the other two sections of the dialog box to make your changes. The Line Types section offers four choices plus a no change option. To add a border, select the line segments to be changed and then click on one of the three line examples. To remove a border, select the line segment and click on the no line option. To change the color of a line, simply select the segment and choose the new color from the Line Color section.

More stuff

If you want to add only a border to the bottom of a cell, you can use the Underline list on the Property Band (the fifth list from the left). If you have a block selected, the border will be put at the bottom of the block, not at the bottom of each individual cell.

If you are using the Active Block dialog box, you continue to see the list of choices to the left of the dialog box. The advantage to the Active Block dialog box is that you can make several types of changes from the same dialog box. The disadvantage is that you cannot see your changes as you make them.

For actually drawing on your notebook pages and your graphs, Quattro Pro has a separate SpeedBar called Draw, which is very easy to use. You can find a discussion of the Draw SpeedBar in the "Toolbar Tour" section.

To find out how to use the formatting commands, see Chapter 12 in *Quattro Pro 6 For Windows For Dummies*.

You can change the background color for a cell by using Active Block⇨Shading. You control whether the gridlines are being displayed by using Active Page⇨Display.

Active Block⇨Numeric Format

Controls the format used for displaying numbers in the selected cell(s). Each cell can have a different format, but, usually, an entire block of cells shares the same format. Basically, you use this feature so that when you type in a number such as 1.1, Quattro Pro displays the number as 1, 1.1000, $1.10, 110%, or a whole bunch of other options.

For mouse maniacs

The Style list, the third list on the Property Band, includes information on the numeric format.

Just the facts

To use a numeric format that is stored as part of a style, simply select the cells and then select the style name from the Style list on the Property Band (third from the left). If you want to modify the format or use one that doesn't appear on the Style list, you need to open the Active Block dialog box.

The mouse method (and my preferred method) to get to the Active Block dialog box to use this command is to select the cell(s) that you want to change, click the right mouse button while the cursor is over the selected cells, and then select (with the left mouse button) the Block Properties choice from the pop-up menu.

The other way to get to the Active Block dialog box is to select your cell(s), select the Property menu on the far right of Property Band (either by clicking on it or by using Alt+P), and then select Current Object. Either method gives you the same dialog box. You then click on Numeric Format in the list on the left.

Most often you will simply choose one of the numeric formats from the list. The table describes what each format does and what other options are available with that format.

Format	*Purpose*	*Other Options*
Fixed	Fixes the number of digits after the decimal so that all the values have the same number of places.	Enter the number of places (for example, enter 3 for thousandths so that 0 would be displayed as 0.000).
Scientific	Changes the number into a single digit followed by a decimal and then indicates how many tens you need to multiply by to get back to the original number (1.2E+2 means 1.2 * 10 * 10 or 120). If the number following the E is negative, you have to divide by that many tens (1.2E-2 means 1.2/10/10 or .012).	Enter the number of places to show after the decimal.
Currency	Puts a currency symbol in front of the number and adds separators every third digit. In the U.S., this means a dollar sign in front and a comma every third digit (such as $1,200,000). In France, the separator is a period (such as 1.200.000). Go figure. Negative numbers are shown within parentheses.	Enter the number of places after the decimal (usually 0 or 2).
Comma	Puts a separator every third digit. In the U.S., the separator is a comma. Other countries use other symbols. Really — trust me. Negative numbers are shown in parentheses.	Enter the number of places after the decimal (usually 0 or 2).
General	If a number fits in the cell without changing it, fine — leave it alone. If the number is too big, see if you can drop some digits after the decimal and round it. If that doesn't work, try showing it in Scientific format. If that doesn't work, give up and display asterisks.	

Format	Purpose	Other Options
+/−	Makes a line for the value of the number using pluses (+) for positive numbers and minuses (−) for negative numbers. A value of 5 would be +++++. A value of −2 would be --. If the number is 0, it shows a decimal point (.).	
Percent	Divides the number by 100 and puts a percent sign (%) at the end.	Enter the number of places to show after the decimal.
Date	Displays numbers as dates in the format you choose.	DD-MMM-YY gives 14-Sep-60; DD-MMM gives 14-Sep; MMM-YY gives Sep-60; Long International gives 09/14/60; Short International gives 09/14.
Time	Displays numbers as times in the format you choose.	HH:MM:SS AM/PM gives 11:59:59PM; HH:MM AM/PM gives 11:59PM; Long International gives 23:59:59; Short International gives 23:59.
Text	Shows the text that makes up the formulas rather than the results.	
Hidden	Doesn't show anything! The cell appears empty, but you can reference the value for use in other formulas.	

The final choice is User Defined, which lets you enter a numeric format by using special secret codes. For codes that display numbers (such as the date), it doesn't matter whether you use lowercase (month) or initial caps (Month) or uppercase (MONTH) when you enter the codes. For codes that display words (such as the day of the week), the way you capitalize the code controls how the results are capitalized.

The first step is to decide whether you are creating a number format (which would start with an *N*) or a date/time format (which would start with a *T*). The secret codes you can use are shown in the following table.

Number Codes

Code	Meaning	Example
0	Required digit. If there isn't a digit in this position in the actual number, the position is filled with a zero (in the front or the back). Causes the number to be rounded to the number of digits after the decimal.	123.456 with a format of N00.00 shows as 123.46; 1 with a format of N00.00 shows as 01.00.
9	Optional digit. Rounds the number to the number of places after the decimal.	123.456 with a format of N99.99 shows as 123.46; 1 with a format of N99.99 shows as 1.00.
, (comma)	Inserts a separator every three places for number codes or where it appears for a date/time format. (The U.S. separator is a comma, but you can change the separator with Application⇨International.)	1000000 with a format of N9,000 shows as 1,000,000; 1 with a format of N9,000 shows as 001.
. (period)	Inserts a decimal separator (a period unless you change it with Application⇨International).	
E– or e–	Scientific notation with either a minus or nothing after the E.	
E+ or e+	Scientific notation with either a minus or a plus after the E.	

Date Codes

Code	Meaning	Example
D	Day of the month as a one- or two-digit number (1 – 31).	
DD	Day of the month as a two-digit number (01 – 31).	
WDAY	Day of the week as a three-character abbreviation that is capitalized the way you enter the code.	wday gives mon; Wday gives Mon; WDAY gives MON.
WEEKDAY	The full name of the day of the week that is capitalized the way you enter the code.	weekday gives monday; Weekday gives Monday; WEEKDAY gives MONDAY.

(continued)

Date Codes

Code	Meaning	Example
Mo	Displays the month as a one- or two-digit number (1 – 12). If not preceded by an H (for hour), you can use a single M.	
MMo	Displays the month as a two-digit number (01 – 12). If not preceded by an H (for hour), you can use MM.	
MON	Displays the month as a three-character abbreviation that is capitalized the way you enter the code.	MON gives JAN; Mon gives Jan; mon gives jan.
MONTH	Displays the full name of the month that is capitalized the way you enter the code.	MONTH gives JANUARY;. Month gives January; month gives january.
YY	Displays the last two digits of the year (00 – 99).	
YYYY	Displays all four digits of the year (0001 – 9999).	

Time codes

Code	Meaning	Example
H	Displays the hour as a one- or two-digit number.	
HH	Displays the hour as a two-digit number.	
AMPM	Causes the hour to be displayed on a 12-hour clock that is capitalized the way you enter the code. Otherwise, military 24-hour time is used. (The codes in the example start with a T because they are time codes.)	Eleven o'clock at night with a format of THAMPM gives 11PM; Eleven o'clock at night with a format of TH gives 23; Eleven o'clock at night with a format of THampm gives 11pm.
Mi	Displays the minute as a one- or two-digit number (1 – 59). If preceded by an hour code (H), you can just use M.	

Code	Meaning	Example
MMi	Displays the minute as a two-digit number (01 – 59). If preceded by an hour code (H), you can use MM.	
s or S	Displays the second as a one- or two-digit number (1 – 59).	
ss or SS	Displays the second as a two-digit number (01 – 59).	

If you decide to create a number format, you can use up to three parts separated by a semicolon (;). The first part is for positive numbers; the second is for negative numbers; and the third is for zero. If you leave out a part, zeros are treated as positive numbers. In addition to the codes shown, you can also include text enclosed in quotation marks (""), which will be inserted exactly as it appears.

More stuff

To learn more about formats, see Chapter 5 in *Quattro Pro 6 For Windows For Dummies*.

You can store a numeric format as part of a style by using Notebook⇨Define Style. For information on entering numbers as labels see the "More stuff" section of Active Block⇨Alignment. The symbols and formats used for currency as well as date and time can be set by using Application⇨International.

Active Block⇨Reveal/Hide

Now you see them, now you don't. This command controls whether or not the selected row(s) or column(s) are hidden. Even though you access this command in the Active Block dialog box, you can't use this command to hide a block of cells. You can hide only entire rows or columns.

Just the facts

The mouse method (and my preferred method) to get to the Active Block dialog box to use this command is to select the cell(s) that you want to change, click the right mouse button while the cursor is over the selected cells, and then select (with the left mouse button) the Block Properties choice from the pop-up menu.

The other method to get to the Active Block dialog box is to select your cell(s), select the Property menu on the far right of the Property Band (either by clicking on it or by using Alt+P), and then select Current Object. Either method gives you the same dialog box. Then select Reveal/Hide from the list on the left.

Now you have some choices to make. First, are you going to work with entire Rows or entire Columns? If you select an entire row or column before opening the dialog box, you don't need to worry. Otherwise, just pick the one you want. Second, are you going to Hide or Reveal the information? If you want, you can always cop out with the No Change choice, but if you pick this option, why did you bother opening the dialog box? Anyway, just click on OK to make your change.

More stuff

To locate a hidden row or column, look carefully at the row numbers or column letters. A missing number or letter indicates a hidden row or column.

To reveal a hidden row, simply select from the row above to the row below (which includes the hidden row) and then set Active Block⇨Reveal/Hide to Reveal all the rows in the selection. Your hidden row jumps right back in.

To hide an entire notebook, use Window⇨Hide. You can disguise the contents of a cell by setting the Active Block⇨Text Color and Active Block⇨Shading options to the same color.

Active Block⇨Row Height

Controls the height of the selected row(s). Wouldn't this be a great feature for people: You gain a little weight, so you just make yourself taller. Wow!

For mouse maniacs

Just put the mouse pointer over the little line between the row numbers and when you see this row-height cursor, drag the line to change the height of the row above the line.

Just the facts

The easiest way to change the height of a row is to place the cursor over the line between the numbers marking the rows and wait for it to turn into the row-height cursor. After you have the right cursor, hold down the mouse button and drag to move the height for the row above the cursor.

More stuff

This is another one of those commands that you can get to by selecting the cell(s) you want to change, clicking the right mouse button while the cursor is over the selected cells, and then selecting (with the left mouse button) the Block Properties choice from the pop-up menu to display the Active Block dialog box. Of course, using the cursor is much easier.

You can reset the height to the default by opening the Active Block dialog box, selecting Reset Height, and then clicking on OK.

If you use the Active Block dialog box, you have greater control and can specify the unit to use for measuring the row height. Your choices are Points, Inches, and Centimeters. A *point* is $1/72$ of an inch and is a very popular term in the publishing industry. Of course, no one else seems to care.

To find out about making those rows taller or shorter, see Chapter 10 in *Quattro Pro 6 For Windows For Dummies*.

To control the vertical alignment, use Active Block ⇨ Alignment. You can also change the width of a column by using Active Block ⇨ Column Width.

Active Block ⇨ Shading

Sets the background shading for the selected cell(s). By using this command, you get a chance to be a great spreadsheet artist. Of course, being creative doesn't do you much good unless people come over and look at your screen or until you buy that expensive color printer. Well, you can use shades of gray, but they're hardly as much fun.

For mouse maniacs

The Shading button on the Format SpeedBar jumps you right to the Shading palette.

Just the facts

The easiest way to use this command is to display the Format SpeedBar by selecting it from the Toolbar list (which is the next to the last list on the Property Band). With the Format SpeedBar displayed, you can select the Shading button to display the Shading dialog box. To use a shade that is already on the palette, simply click on the color you want in the Color 1 section and then click on the far left square in the Blend section. When you click on OK (or press Return), the background of the selected cell(s) changes to that shade.

Using a blended color is a bit more complicated, but not much. To use a blended color, pick the starting color in the Color 1 section and the ending color in the Color 2 section. The Blend section now contains a series of seven shades ranging from the starting color to the ending color. To use a shade for the background color, simply click on it and then choose OK.

More stuff

If the Format SpeedBar isn't showing, use the mouse method (and my preferred method) to get to the Active Block dialog box to use this command. Select the cell(s) that you want to change, click the right mouse button while the cursor is over the selected cells, and then select (with the left mouse button) the Block Properties choice from the pop-up menu.

The other method to get to the Active Block dialog box is to select your cell(s), select the Property menu on the far right of Property Band (either by clicking on it or by using Alt+P), and then select Current Object. Either method gives you the same dialog box where you can select Shading from the list on the left.

Use Active Notebook⇨Palette to change the available colors. Because Quattro Pro remembers the shades you use based upon their position within the palette, making changes to the palette can cause already formatted cells to change color.

Although you can hide the contents of a cell by using Active Block⇨Numeric Format and assigning the Hidden format to the cell, an even cooler method is to make the text color and the background color the same.

To control the appearance of the cell's borders (including their color), use Active Block⇨Line Drawing. To control the color of text within the cell, use Active Block⇨Text Color. You can record all these settings as part of a style by using Notebook⇨Define Style.

Active Block⇨Text Color

Sets the color for the text in the selected cell(s).

For mouse maniacs

If the Format SpeedBar is displayed, one click on the Text Color button takes you right to the Text Color options.

Just the facts

Make sure that the Format SpeedBar is displayed. If it's not, select it from the Toolbar list (the next to the last list on the Property Band). You can then select the block to be changed, click on the Text Color button, select a color, and click on OK.

More stuff

The mouse method (and my preferred method) to get to the Active Block dialog box to use this command is to select the cell(s) that you want to change, click the right mouse button while the cursor is over the selected cells, and then select (with the left mouse button) the Block Properties choice from the pop-up menu.

The other method to get to the Active Block dialog box is to select your cell(s), select the Property menu on the far right of the Property Band (either by clicking on it or by using Alt+P), and then select Current Object. Either method gives you the same dialog box where you can select Text Color from the list on the left.

You can hide text by setting the Text Color and the Shading options to the same color. This technique can be useful for hiding values that you use in formulas or for smuggling secret messages into Florida.

The colors that are available in the dialog box are controlled by the Active Notebook⇨Palette command. The colors are assigned by position . If you format a bunch of cells with the color in the lower-right corner and then change that color, all the cells you already formatted will also change to that color.

To change the look of the characters within the cell, use Active Block⇨Font. To change the background color, use Active Block⇨Shading. You can set the default color for three different value ranges by using Active Page⇨Conditional Color.

Active Notebook dialog box

Many of Quattro Pro's commands are not found on the menus, but rather on dialog boxes that are gotten to either by using the right mouse button or the Property menu on the far right of the Property Band. The Active Notebook commands are one example of this type of dialog box. There are two ways to get to the Active Notebook dialog box. The one I prefer requires that you work with the notebook in a window that is not maximized. This means that the filename for the notebook appears in the title bar of its own window rather than up with the application's name. If the notebook is in its own window, point to its titlebar and click the right mouse button. The other method is to open the Property menu at the far right end of the Property Band (you can use Alt, P) and select Active Notebook.

When you are looking at the dialog box, you'll notice a list of choices along the left side. To select among the various options on the dialog box, click on the command you want to work with. For example, to use the dialog box to change the palette for the notebook, you would position your cursor over the word "Palette" and click once with the left button. The rest of dialog box changes to the controls for that command. Wish it were less confusing, but I barely had time to write the book let alone rewrite the program.

Active Notebook⇨Display

Controls whether you see the scroll bars or page tabs for the current notebook as well as how objects are displayed. These settings are stored with the notebook.

Just the facts

If the notebook is displayed in its own window (a smaller window within the application window), you can click on the notebook's title bar with the right mouse button to display the Active Notebook dialog box. (If you end up with the Application dialog box instead, you clicked on the wrong title bar. The notebook probably wasn't in its own window.)

If the notebook isn't in its own window (or you prefer to use another method), simply select the Property list on the far right of the Property Band and then select Active Notebook. Both methods take you to the same dialog box. In the Active Notebook dialog box, select Display from the list on the left.

The Display section controls whether the current notebook displays a Vertical Scroll Bar (along the right side), a Horizontal Scroll Bar (along the bottom), both scroll bars, or neither scroll bar. If the box next to the item is checked, it is displayed on-screen. If the check box is cleared, the item doesn't appear on the notebook pages. If you don't display scroll bars, you can still use the Edit⇨Go to command to get around or use the keyboard keys. The other item in the Display group is Page Tabs. If you get rid of the page tabs, the only way to see what page you are on is by checking the cell indicator on the input line.

The Objects section determines how objects, such as graphs, that you have placed on your notebook pages are displayed. If you select Show Qutline, all you see is the outline of the object's shape (usually a rectangle). If you select Hide, you don't see anything where you've placed an object. Use Show All to have the object displayed normally.

More stuff

If you don't have scroll bars or page tabs, you will get a lot of use out of your Page Up and Page Down keys. Use Ctrl+Page Up to move to the preceding page and Ctrl+Page Down to move to the next page. By themselves, Page Up and Page Down move you up and down a full screen of cells. Use Ctrl+left arrow to move a full screen to the left and Ctrl+right arrow to move a full screen to the right.

Other general display settings are found under Application⇨Display. You can use the View⇨Display command to change any of display settings for the active notebook or application. You can also display or hide parts of the current page by using Active Page⇨Display.

Active Notebook⇨Macro Library

Makes the notebook into a macro library. You probably won't use this command very often, but it is useful after you start writing your own collection of macros.

Just the facts

Even though you probably won't use this command, you should know how to get to it. If the notebook is displayed in its own window (a smaller window within the application window), you can click on the notebook's title bar with the right mouse button to display the Active Notebook dialog box. (If you end up with the Application dialog box, you clicked on the wrong title bar. The notebook probably wasn't in its own window.)

If the notebook isn't in its own window (or you prefer to use another method), simply select the Property list on the far right of the Property Band and then select Active Notebook. Both methods take you to the same dialog box. In the Active Notebook dialog box, select Macro Library from the list on the left.

At this point, you have two choices: Yes (make the active notebook into a macro library) and No (make the active notebook into a normal notebook).

More stuff

A macro library is a notebook that serves as a holding place for all your macros. Instead of having to place a copy of the macro into the active notebook, you can place the macro into the macro library, where it can be shared by all the opened notebooks. The only requirement is that the notebook containing the macro library must be one of your opened notebooks. You may want to hide the library (with Window⇨Hide) and then automatically load it as part of a workspace (File⇨Workspace).

You can arrange to have a macro library load automatically by using the Application⇨File Options dialog box, which gives you a method for creating a notebook — full of your favorite macros — that is always available while you work. To make sure that the notebook doesn't get closed by mistake, make it a system notebook, as well.

To learn what you need to know about Macros, see Chapter 18 in *Quattro Pro 6 For Windows For Dummies*.

To create a macro library, you need to have created macros by using Tools⇨Macro. You may want to hide the library by using Window⇨Hide. You also may want to make the library into a system notebook, which makes it harder for someone to close it accidentally.

Active Notebook⇨Palette

Controls what colors are available for use with such commands as Shading and Text Color. Using this command is your chance to design your own custom colors and then coordinate your office to match.

Just the facts

If the notebook is being displayed in its own window (a smaller window within the application window), you can click on the notebook's title bar with the right mouse button to display the Active Notebook dialog box. (If you end up with the Application dialog box, you clicked on the wrong title bar. The notebook probably wasn't in its own window.)

If the notebook isn't in its own window (or you prefer to use another method), simply select the Property list on the far right of the Property Band and then select Active Notebook. Both methods take you to the same dialog box. In the Active Notebook dialog box, click on the Palette option in the list on the left, and you are ready to go.

The palette has slots for 16 colors organized in a 4-by-4 grid. (For those of you following along on your computer, there really is a slot in the second position on the top row — it just matches the background.) You can change the color contained in any of the slots by clicking on the slot and then selecting Edit Color. The Edit Palette Color dialog box appears, where you can select a replacement color from the 4-by-14 grid (a total of 56 colors). You can also change any of the colors on the grid by clicking on its slot and then using the scroll bars at the bottom of the dialog box to change the mix of colors. After you pick your new color, select OK, and you're returned to the palette. You can either make additional changes or select OK to return to your work. (It's more fun to make up new colors than it is to work!)

You can return to the original palette by going to Active Notebook⇨Palette and selecting Reset Defaults. This action resets all the slots, not just the one you have selected.

More stuff

To change the background color for all cells on all pages, change the color in the upper-left corner (white by default).

The palette is used by such commands as Active Block⇨Text Color, Active Block⇨Shading, and Active Page⇨Conditional Color. In fact, the palette is used by any command that sets the color of objects (including Active Block⇨Line Drawing).

Active Notebook⇨Password Level

Sets a password for the current notebook. You can require a password to view the formulas (Low security), view the notebook (Medium security), or even to load the notebook (High security).

Just the facts

If the notebook is being displayed in its own window (a smaller window within the application window), you can click on the notebook's title bar with the right mouse button to display the Active Notebook dialog box. (If you end up with the Application dialog box, you clicked on the wrong title bar. The notebook probably wasn't in its own window.)

If the notebook isn't in its own window (or you prefer to use another method), simply select the Property list on the far right of the Property Band and then select Active Notebook. Both methods take you to the same dialog box. In the Active Notebook dialog box, simply click on the Password Level option in the list on the left, and then you can set the level of security you want.

There are four possible levels of security: None, Low (which requires the password in order to view formulas), Medium (which requires the password in order to view the notebook), and High (which requires the password to open the notebook). Choose a level and then click on OK. You are asked to enter a password. Click on OK. You are asked to enter a password. Click on OK. (You really do have to do this procedure twice — and the passwords you enter must match.)

When you are returned to the notebook, it will seem like nothing happened. In order to see the security in effect, you need to close the notebook and reopen it. Be sure that you don't forget the password.

More stuff

There's another way to set the highest level of protection. When you use File⇨Save As, a dialog box appears where you can enter a password in the Protection Password text box without having to use the Active Notebook dialog box.

With low security, you can still make changes to the formulas. If you want to prevent other people from making changes to your notebook, you should use Active Page⇨Protection.

Unfortunately, if you apply a password with low or medium security, it's a real pain to undo your work. The Password Level option disappears from the Active Notebook dialog box. To enter the password, you must exit Quattro Pro and then restart by executing a special command. One way to restart is with File⇨Run in the Program Manager. You have to know the location of Quattro Pro, the name and location of the notebook file, and, of course, the password. With all this information, you're ready to start. First, type the location of Quattro Pro, a backslash (\) and QPW, without any spaces between the parts. Then type a space followed by the location and name of the notebook (something like C:\DATA\IWANTIN.WB2). Finally, type another space, a slash (/), an uppercase letter S and then the password — all without any spaces. Now when you click on OK, Quattro Pro should start and load the notebook without any password security.

It's hard to come up with good passwords (and it's good to come up with hard-to-guess passwords). The most important thing is to make sure that you remember the password when you need it. One trick that works for me is to use capital letters within the word where they don't usually belong. Then if someone guesses the password, he or she still has to figure out which letters are capitals. Another option is to either insert numbers into the middle of the word or tack them on to either end. A final suggestion is to replace such letters as O, I, and L with the digits 0 (zero) and 1 (one).

Use Active Page⇨Protection and Active Block⇨Constraints to
control what cells are available for input.

Active Notebook⇨Recalc Settings

Tells Quattro Pro when to recalculate your formulas. If the
notebook takes forever to update after you change a value, you
may want to change the recalculation method. You can also
control how the recalculations are done. You also use this
command to look for clues about any circular references in your
worksheet.

Just the facts

If the notebook is being displayed in its own window (a smaller
window within the application window), you can click on the
notebook's title bar with the right mouse button to display the
Active Notebook dialog box. (If you end up with the Application
dialog box, you clicked on the wrong title bar. The notebook
probably wasn't in its own window.)

If the notebook isn't in its own window (or you prefer to use
another method), simply select the Property list on the far right
of the Property Band and then select Active Notebook. Both
methods take you to the Active Notebook dialog box, where you
can select Recalc Settings from the list on the left.

The most common use for this dialog box is to change when the
recalculations are performed. Normally, the Background choice is
selected. With it, Quattro Pro automatically recalculates all your
formulas when you make changes, but only when nothing else
seems to be going on. Your other choices are Manual and
Automatic. To change the setting, select one of the choices and
then click on OK.

The Automatic setting pauses and recalculates each formula after
you change the contents of any cell. The difference between
Automatic and Background usually isn't noticeable on a fast
system. If you have a lot of formulas, however, Automatic mode
can really slow things down. On a slow system, on the other
hand, the Background setting may not have enough time between
your actions to finish the recalculations.

If you seem to spend all your time waiting for the recalculations
to finish, go ahead and select Manual mode. With Manual mode
(or when Background mode runs out of time), you are responsible for telling Quattro Pro when to recalculate by pressing F9.

Quattro Pro reminds you to recalculate by displaying the code CACL in the status bar at the bottom of the screen. By the way, when you first enter a formula with <u>M</u>anual mode, Quattro Pro goes ahead and calculates the result for you by using the current values in the notebook. Unfortunately, the other values may not be correct if they contained formulas that needed to be updated!

The other settings in this dialog box are for advanced features. The choices in the Order section control which formulas Quattro Pro calculates first. <u>C</u>olumn-wise starts with the left column and works across the page. <u>R</u>ow-wise starts at the top and works down. <u>N</u>atural, the normal setting, calculates those formulas that are based only on values, then those that are based only on values and on formulas that were calculated in the first pass, and then any formulas that reference formulas calculated in the second pass, and so on. Unless your notebook contains circular references that you need to calculate, the order doesn't matter, and you should use <u>N</u>ormal. (Circular references are explained in the second tip in the "More stuff" section.)

If you do need to use circular references, the # of <u>I</u>terations setting works with <u>R</u>ow-wise and <u>C</u>olumn-wise order and controls whether Quattro Pro goes back and checks whether calculating the results of a formula changed the results for any formulas in a preceding row or column. The value in # of <u>I</u>terations tells Quattro Pro how many times to check. Unless you know why you are changing them, leave the Order and # of <u>I</u>terations settings alone.

If you are having trouble figuring out why a formula doesn't calculate, you may want to turn on Audit <u>E</u>rrors. With this option on, Quattro Pro displays the cell that contains the source of the error as the result for each cell that it cannot calculate. You may have to make your columns wider in order to see the cell name that is displayed. This option doesn't help you if your formulas are working but are giving you the incorrect answers. That's what office gurus are for!

The Compile <u>F</u>ormulas check box can speed up the calculations in certain types of notebooks on systems with a math coprocessor. To find out if there is any advantage for you in checking Compile <u>F</u>ormulas, use the Performance expert under <u>H</u>elp⇨<u>E</u>xperts.

More stuff

If you are working in <u>M</u>anual mode and want to force a single formula to recalculate, you can move to the formula, double-click on the cell, and then press Return.

TIP

One of the problems that people run into when writing formulas is that they make their formulas *circular*. A circular set of formulas is one in which the first formula in the chain refers forward to the last. With a circular formula, you can never find the correct answer because you don't know what the answer will be in the last cell when you have to calculate the first one.

Imagine, for example, that you have two formulas: cell A1 contains the formula A2 + 1, and cell A2 contains the formula A1 + 1. When you enter the formula in cell A1, Quattro Pro checks cell A2, finds out that it's empty (and has a value of zero), and puts 1 as the result of the formula in cell A1. You then enter the formula in cell A2, and Quattro Pro checks cell A1, sees that it holds a value of 1 (from the first formula), and puts 2 as the result of the formula in cell A2. But, wait, the result in cell A1 is suddenly wrong because cell A2 now holds the value 2, not the value 0, as it did when you started. So Quattro Pro updates cell A1 to read 3. OK, but now cell A2 is wrong because A1 contains 3 instead of the 1 it did a minute ago. This recalculation can go on and on and is referred to as a set of circular references.

When Quattro Pro detects a circular reference, it updates the formula only once and displays the code CIRC in the status bar at the bottom of the screen. If you go to the Active Notebook⇨Recalc Settings screen, you find a list of cells that contain a circular reference. (This may or may not be the cell you have to change. Quattro Pro lists only one cell out of each set of circular references.) By the way, if you really need a set of circular references, you can control how many times Quattro Pro goes back and forth by using the # of Iterations setting on the Active Notebook⇨Recalc Settings dialog box.)

Active Notebook⇨System

Turns the current notebook into a System notebook. If you know what this means, go for it. Otherwise, leave it alone. Yes, I know what it means, but my contract explicitly prevents me from providing details.

Just the facts

If the notebook is being displayed in its own window (a smaller window within the application window), you can click on the notebook's title bar with the right mouse button to display the Active Notebook dialog box. (If you end up with the Application dialog box, you clicked on the wrong title bar. The notebook probably wasn't in its own window.)

If the notebook isn't in its own window (or you prefer to use another method), simply select the Property list on the far right of the Property Band and then select Active Notebook. Both methods take you to the Active Notebook dialog box where you can select System from the list on the left of the notebook.

You have only two choices: Yes (make it a system notebook) and No (make a regular, plain notebook). The advantage of a system notebook is that it is harder for someone to accidentally close it. This can be useful, especially if it contains macros or values that you need to use in another notebook.

More stuff

The two types of notebooks that are most often made into system notebooks are ones that contain values or formulas that are common to other notebooks and those that contain macro libraries. For more on macro libraries, see Active Notebook⇨Macro Library.

Active Notebook⇨Zoom Factor

Sets the default zoom factor for pages in the notebook. The higher the zoom factor, the bigger the letters.

Just the facts

If the notebook is being displayed in its own window (a smaller window within the application window), you can click on the notebook's title bar with the right mouse button to display the Active Notebook dialog box. (If you end up with the Application dialog box, you clicked on the wrong title bar. The notebook probably wasn't in its own window.)

If the notebook isn't in its own window (or you prefer to use another method), simply select the Property list on the far right of the Property Band and then select Active Notebook. Both methods take you to the Active Notebook dialog box.

Select Zoom Factor from the list on the left, select a value from the list that is now on the right, and then click on OK. You've done it! You've set a default zoom factor for the notebook. Now go to any page where you haven't already changed the zoom factor to see what it looks like.

More stuff

The Selection option is most useful when you are setting the Active Page⇨Zoom Factor. To use this option, select a block before opening the dialog box. After choosing Selection and OK, the magnification of the block will be adjusted until it takes up the entire work area on-screen.

To set the magnification for a single page, use Active Page⇨Zoom Factor. It even has a shortcut! (Select the zoom factor directly from the list on the Property Band.)

Active Page dialog box

Far too many of Quattro Pro's commands are not found on the menus, but rather on dialog boxes that are gotten to either by using the right mouse button or the Property menu on the far right of the Property Band. The Active Page commands are one example of this type of dialog box. There are two ways to get to the Active Page dialog box. The easy one is to point to the page tab and click the right mouse button. The other is to open the Property menu at the far right end of the Property Band (you can use Alt, P) and select Active Page.

When you are looking at the dialog box, you'll notice a list of choices along the left side. To select among the various options on the dialog box, click on the command you want to work with. For example, to use the dialog box to change the color of the page's tab, you would position your cursor over the words "Tab Color" and click once with the left button. The rest of dialog box changes to the controls for that command. It's confusing, it's strange, it's Quattro Pro!

Active Page⇨Conditional Color

Sets the color for three different groups of values plus error conditions. You create the three groups by entering the "smallest normal value" and the "largest normal value." The three groups are as follows: below the smallest normal value, between the two values, and above the largest normal value. The values you enter are included in the middle (normal) group.

Just the facts

To get to the Active Page dialog box, simply click on the page tab with the right mouse button. Or, if you prefer, you can go to the Property menu at the far right of the Property Band and select Active Page from the list.

Select Conditional Color from the list on the left of the Active Page dialog box. To set the color for the ERR message that appears in cells that have formulas that cannot be calculated, simply select the ERR Color option, select a color from the palette, and, assuming you don't want to make any other changes, select OK.

To set the conditional colors, there are three steps. First, turn the feature on by placing a check in the Enable check box. Next, enter values for the Smallest Normal Value and the Greatest Normal Value. These are the smallest and largest values allowed within the normal range. The third step is to assign colors to the three groups by using the palette grid. Notice that the name of the grid changes, based upon which item is selected in the Options group.

The color for values within the normal range (which includes the smallest and greatest values) is set by clicking on the Normal Color option and picking a color from the grid. To set the color for values below the Smallest Normal Value, click on the Below Normal Color option and pick a color from the grid. To assign a color for those values above the Greatest Normal Value, click on the Above Normal Color option and pick a color from the grid. After you select OK to leave the dialog box, the values in your notebook will be color-coded based on which of the three groups they belong to — below the Smallest Normal Value, within the normal range, or above the Greatest Normal Value.

More stuff

You can directly specify a color for the text in a cell by using Active Block⇨Text Color.

Active Page⇨Default Width

Sets the default column width. The default width is the one that you start out with for every column on the page. This setting has no effect on column widths that you have set for individual columns.

Just the facts

To get to the Active Page dialog box, simply click on the page tab with the right mouse button. Or, if you prefer, you can go to the Property menu at the far right of the Property Band and select Active Page from the list. Click on Default Width in the list on the left, and you are ready to enter the column width.

First, select the units — Characters, Inches, or Centimeters. Next, enter the value for the Column Width. Finally, select OK and watch the columns change width.

More stuff

Be aware that the Characters measurement doesn't really have anything to do with how many characters you can fit into the cell. It used to be that an *I* and a *W* both used the same amount of space (a *monospaced* font). Now, most fonts are *proportional,* which means that each character can have its own width. Using a proportional font means that you can fit more *I*s into a cell than *W*s. Fortunately, as a unit, a *character* always means the same thing — approximately 0.17 inch.

To change the width for a single column (or a group of columns), you use Active Block⇨Column Width. You can also change the height by using Active Block⇨Row Height.

Active Page⇨Display

Controls whether you see the row numbers, column letters, the gridlines between cells, and the contents of cells that have a value of zero. This command is most useful for removing gridlines so that you can see the borders that you put in by using the Active Block⇨Line Drawing command.

Just the facts

To get to the Active Page dialog box, simply click on the page tab with the right mouse button. Or, if you prefer, you can go to the Property menu at the far right of the Property Band and select Active Page from the list. Select Display from the list on the left, and you're ready to go.

The Display Zero options are Yes (which means to show a 0 in cells with a value of zero) and No (which means to empty out cells with a value of zero and leave blank any cell with a formula with a result of zero).

The Borders options refer to the column letters across the top and the row numbers down the side. To remove these letters and numbers from your screen, clear the check from the Row Borders check box to remove the numbers, from the Column Borders check box to remove the letters, or from both check boxes to remove both borders.

The Grid Lines choices refer to the lines that appear between the cells on your page. Remove the check from the Vertical check box to remove the gridlines between columns and from the Horizontal check box to remove the gridlines from between rows.

More stuff

You can control what else is shown on-screen by using View⇨Display. If you want to have lines between the cells that you can format, use Active Block⇨Line Drawing.

Active Page⇨Name

Gives the page a name, which makes it much easier to remember what information you put on that page. For example, you will find it easier to remember to list your paycheck on the Income page rather than on page F.

Just the facts

Although it's possible to assign a page name by using the Active Page dialog box, it's much easier to click on the page tab with the left mouse button and just type the new name. Press Return when you are done.

More stuff

If you insist on using the Active Page dialog box, however, simply click on the page tab with the right mouse button and select Name from the list on the left. Or, if you prefer, you can go to the Property menu at the far right of the Property Band, select Active Page from the list, and then select Name.

To learn how to get the most out of your notebooks, see Chapter 14 in *Quattro Pro 6 For Windows For Dummies*.

If you have named your pages, you may also want to name the blocks of cells by using Block⇨Names.

Active Page⇨Protection

Turns the cell protection on or off for the entire page. With cell protection active, you can enter information only into cells that have been unprotected by using the Active Block⇨Constraints command.

Just the facts

To get to the Active Page dialog box, simply click on the page tab with the right mouse button. Or, if you prefer, you can go to the Property menu at the far right of the Property Band and select Active Page from the list. Select Protection from the list on the left, and you're ready to lock things down.

To protect the page from having someone enter things into cells, put a check next to the Enable Cell Locking check box and click on OK. Now when anyone tries to enter information into a cell, he or she sees a message that that action is not allowed. To open up a block of cells so that it is available for imput while the rest of the page is protected, select the block and use Active Block⇨Constraints.

To prevent changes to the objects (such things as a graph placed upon a page) in your notebook, put a check mark next to the Enable Object Locking check box and click on OK.

More stuff

Unfortunately, it's very easy for someone to undo the protection you have put on your notebook. Protection is really intended to prevent the accidental destruction of a formula while you are doing data entry.

Whether you unprotect the cells before or after you put on page protection is a matter of personal preference. One trick that makes it easier to see what you're doing is to select all the cells you want to unprotect at one time. If there are several different blocks, select the first block and then hold down the Ctrl key while you highlight the remaining blocks. This trick lets you see all the cells that you intend to unprotect. To finish up, put the cursor over one of the selected cells, click the right mouse button, select Block Properties (which opens the Active Block dialog box), and then choose Constraints.

To unprotect cells so that you can put things in them, use Active Block⇨Constraints. If you want to have cells that are available only for input (in other words, you can't format them or use other commands), you first unprotect them with Active Block⇨Constraints and then use Block⇨Restrict Input.

Active Page⇨Tab Color

Sets the color of the active page's tab. This is one of those unusual commands that does exactly what it sounds like.

Just the facts

To get to the Active Page dialog box, simply click on the page tab with the right mouse button. Or, if you prefer, you can go to the Property menu at the far right of the Property Band and select Active Page from the list. You now want to select Tab Color from the list on the left.

For some reason, Quattro Pro gives you more choices for your tab color than for most things. Rather than the 16 choices in the palette, you get a full 56 choices on the color grid. You also have the option of changing any of the colors by using the slider bars at the bottom of the screen. To change the tab color, simply click on one of the colors, make any changes, and click on OK.

More stuff

The colors on the grid are shared by the entire Quattro Pro program. If you make changes to a color that is already being used by another tab, you will also change that tab's color.

To change the name on the tab, use Active Page⇨Name.

Active Page⇨Zoom Factor

Sets the zoom factor for the active page, which is a fancy way of saying that it controls how big the information is on-screen. A higher zoom factor means that the text and even the actual cells are bigger.

For mouse maniacs

The list on the Property Band that has a bunch of percentages (third from the right) is the Zoom Factor list. You can use it to set the zoom factor for the current page.

Just the facts

The easiest way to use this command is with the Zoom Factor list on the Property Band. (It's the one that has a percentage value showing, third from the right.) To change the Zoom Factor, just pick a new value from the list.

More stuff

Perhaps the most useful Zoom Factor is Selection. To use it, highlight a block and then choose Selection from the Zoom Factor list. The selected block is enlarged or reduced as necessary to fill up the entire work area. This trick makes it really easy to focus on your work.

If for some reason you don't want to use the Zoom Factor list on the Property Band, you get to the Active Page dialog box by simply clicking on the page tab with the right mouse button. Or, if you prefer, you can go to the Property menu at the far right of the Property Band and select Active Page from the list.

To change the magnification for all the pages, use Active Notebook⇨Zoom Factor.

Application dialog box

A number of Quattro Pro's commands are not found on the menus, but rather on dialog boxes that are gotten to either by using the right mouse button or the Property menu on the far right of the Property Band. The Application commands are one example of this type of dialog box. You won't find an Active Block choice on any of the menus and, in fact, is the one dialog box that you must use the right mouse button to get to. To open the Application dialog box, click the right mouse button over the program's title bar (up where it says "Novell Quattro Pro").

When you are looking at the dialog box, you'll notice a list of choices along the left side. To select among the various options on the dialog box, click on the command you want to work with. For example, to use the dialog box to change the settings for international customization, you would position your cursor over the word "International" and click once with the left button. The rest of dialog box changes to the controls for that command. It's actually quite easy once you've done it once or twice.

Application⇨Display

Controls what parts of the application you see on-screen. Your choices include the Property Band, the current toolbar (SpeedBar), the input line, and several others. You can also control whether Quattro Pro displays the current time in the lower-left corner of the screen — a very important consideration because you wouldn't want to miss your afternoon coffee break!

Just the facts

To get to the Application dialog box, simply click on the application title bar (up where it says Quattro Pro) with the right mouse button.

The Application⇨Display dialog box has three sections, but the most important is the one labeled Display Options. The easiest way to see what these settings refer to is to look at the figure I've thoughtfully provided.

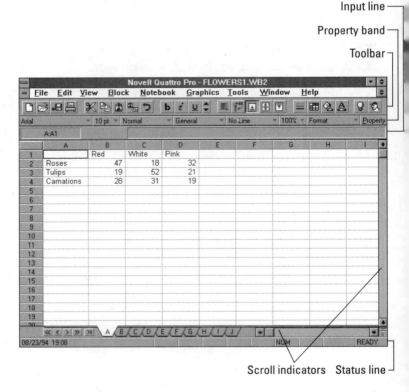

Input line

Property band

Toolbar

Scroll indicators   Status line

If there is a check next to an item on the list, it is shown on-screen. If the check box is cleared, then the item doesn't show on-screen. (The other item in the Display Options list, Balloon Hints, refers to the little box that appears when you hold your cursor over a button. For more information on using this feature, see Help⇨Identify Button or List.)

The Clock Display section offers three choices. None doesn't display any clock on the status bar. Standard displays the date and time in the lower-left corner of the screen (on the status bar) with the format 14-Sep-94 11:59 PM. The International choice uses the same spot, but the format 09/14/94 23:59.

The final section, 3-D Syntax, has two choices. You have to pick one or the other. A..B:A1..B1 shows the page range at the start of the reference followed by the cell range. A:A1..B:B1 puts the page for the first cell and its cell address and then the page for the second cell and its cell address. Which choice you use is a matter of preference, although the first option is the default and is used most often.

More stuff

Other parts of the screen are controlled by Active Notebook⇨Display, and other parts are controlled by Active Page⇨Display.

Application⇨File Options

Used to activate the automatic backup feature and to set the time between backups. Other than that, you should probably leave the settings in this dialog box alone.

Just the facts

To get to the Application dialog box, simply click on the application title bar (up where it says Quattro Pro) with the right mouse button. To change this group of settings, you need to select File Options from the list on the left.

Perhaps the most useful feature is the Auto-backup. Use the number box to enter the time in minutes between automatic backups. (A *backup* is a second copy of the file that you are working on that is stored separately for safekeeping.) To turn on this feature, simply put a check next to the Activate check box. After you click on OK, Quattro Pro starts timing, and after however many minutes you requested, it pauses and saves a copy of your file.

You can use the Directory text box to enter the name of the directory where Quattro Pro should look for notebooks. If you want to have a notebook load automatically when Quattro Pro starts, enter its name in the Autoload File text box.

The Enable Full Path Titles option causes Quattro Pro to display the directory information along with any filenames. This option helps you organize your files because you always know where a file is located, but all the extra letters make the filename harder to read. To turn on the feature, just make sure that the check box has a check in it.

For those of you that prefer the look and feel of WordPerfect over Windows, you can check the WordPerfect file dialogs option. If you are using Perfect Office, this feature can make things a little bit less confusing.

More stuff

 I hid the discussion of the File Extension text box down here because it is the most dangerous. You can use this option to change the three-letter extension that Quattro Pro puts on the end of files — which is a bad idea because changing the file extension makes it more difficult to identify the files created by Quattro Pro 6. Changing the extension may also make it more difficult to find files because Quattro Pro uses the first letter of the extension to decide what files to list in the Open dialog box. The normal extension for Quattro Pro 6 is .WB2.

 A particularly useful trick involving the Autoload File option is to list the name of a macro library. A *macro library* is a collection of macros that are available to other notebooks when the macro library is open. By listing a macro library as the Autoload File, you ensure that it will always be available for your use.

 You can control the way in which a single file is stored by using File⇔Save As.

Application⇔General

A collection of important settings that didn't fit anywhere else. These settings include whether the Undo feature is active, whether you move down a cell when you press Return (or whether you just sit there), how long it takes to activate drag-and-drop editing, and a few others. All in all, a very useful collection of settings.

Just the facts

To get to the Application dialog box, simply click on the application title bar (up where it says Quattro Pro) with the right mouse button. Select General from the list on the left to see your options.

Undo Enabled controls whether the Undo feature is activated. Unless the performance is so slow on your system that you can't bear it, leave this option checked. Even with bad performance, the time factor is a toss-up between whether you lose more time waiting for your computer or correcting a mistake that could have been easily undone if the feature were on.

Compatible Keys makes Quattro Pro pretend that it's the DOS version of the program. Why you wouldn't have just bought the DOS version is beyond me, but it's a feature.

Move Cell Selector on Enter Key controls what happens when you press the Return or Enter key. If this option is checked, you move down a cell; otherwise, you just kind of sit there.

Save Toolbars on Exit can be used to store your favorite arrangement of toolbars. To use this option, arrange the SpeedBar (toolbars) the way you want, open the dialog box, turn on the feature, select OK, and exit Quattro Pro. The only trick is remembering to turn the feature off so that you don't save a different arrangement by mistake!

Cell Drag and Drop Delay Time (ms) controls how long you have to wait after selecting a block and holding the pointer over it before the cursor turns into the little grasping hand which indicates that you can drag the block to a new location. Five hundred milliseconds (ms) is equal to one-half of a second.

More stuff

Other categories that control settings are listed as entries under Active Notebook, Active Page, and Application.

Application⇨International

Lets you choose the default formats for currency format, numeric punctuation, date and time formats, and the language used by Spell Check and other language features. This feature is great for people who have to change nationalities often.

Just the facts

To get to the Application dialog box, simply click on the application title bar (up where it says Quattro Pro) with the right mouse button. Click on International (on the list on the left) to see one of the most complex dialog boxes ever designed. Apparently the programmers thought that if you could master another culture, computers could hold no secrets.

The Selection section on the left side consists of a list of five options. The contents of the right side change for each option.

The most important option within Currency is the choice you must make between using the Windows Default and the settings within Quattro Pro. If you select Windows Default, the rest of the choices disappear because you have just indicated that you want to use the settings from Windows, not the ones from this dialog box. Assuming that you're using the Quattro Pro settings, however, your next choice is what to use as the Currency Symbol and whether to place the symbol before the number (Prefix) or after the number (Suffix). The final choice for Currency is whether negative numbers are shown with a minus sign (Signed) or enclosed in parentheses (Parens).

Punctuation provides a list of three punctuation options for numbers and cell references. You must first choose which symbol to use to mark the decimal (in the U.S., we use a period). Then you must choose which symbol to use to separate the thousandths (in the U.S., we use a comma). Finally, you must choose which symbol to use to separate cells or blocks within cell addresses. Your choices are a period, a comma, or a semi-colon (;). As with the Currency option, you can just decide to use the Windows Default.

Both Date Format and Time Format give you a list of choices with a long format followed by a short format. For help in deciphering the codes, see the information under Active Block⇨Number Format. As with the other options, you can just decide to use the Windows Default for either or both.

The final category is Language, which lets you select the language and, hence, the dictionary for such features as Spell Check. Of course, there's always ye olde Windows Default option.

The LICS option is of interest only if you are converting Lotus 1-2-3 WK1 files that use the Lotus International Character Set. If you need this option, I assume you know what it all means. For those who care about such things, Lotus came up with its own alphabet, and this option makes sure that the characters get converted correctly when you abandon 1-2-3 and move to Quattro Pro.

More stuff

You can set the format for values in a cell or group of cells by using Active Block⇨Numeric Format.

Application⇨Macro

Lets you speed up your macros by telling Quattro Pro not to bother redrawing the screen while the macro is running. You can also set which macro is used at start-up and which menus are displayed when you press the slash (/) key.

Just the facts

To get to the Application dialog box, simply click on the application title bar (up where it says Quattro Pro) with the right mouse button. To get the correct dialog box, you select Macro from the list on the left.

The Suppress-Redraw options control what parts of the screen Quattro Pro tries to redraw while running a macro. The Both option (the default) means that Quattro Pro doesn't bother with much of anything. If you select Panel, Quattro Pro won't redraw menus, dialog boxes, the input line, or the status bar, but it will try to redraw windows and their contents. If you select Window, Quattro Pro won't redraw windows or anything in them, but it will try to draw most of the surrounding real estate (such as menus, input lines, status bars, and so on). If you select None, Quattro Pro will try to redraw the entire screen, which may slow down the execution of your macro.

The Slash Key controls what happens when you press the slash key (/) to activate the alternative menu set. The standard choices are between Lotus 1-2-3 and Quattro Pro for DOS.

The Startup Macro lets you enter the name of the macro to be run when Quattro Pro first starts or when you open a new notebook. For a macro to run when Quattro Pro first starts, you must have started Quattro Pro with a notebook already loaded (by including a notebook name on the command line, by naming a notebook to automatically load, or by double-clicking on a notebook to start the program).

More stuff

You can store an entire notebook of macros by using Active Notebook⇨Macro Library. If you want to automatically run a macro when you start Quattro Pro, use Active Notebook⇨File Options to designate an Auto-Load file.

Block Properties (See Active Block)

The Block Properties command only appears on the pop-up menu that appears when you click the right mouse button over the cells on your notebook page. Selecting Block Properties opens the Active Block dialog box. Because there are so many features that can be set by using this dialog box, it has its own group of entries under Active Block⇨*Command Name*. Of course, instead of *Command Name*, you'll find the setting from the dialog box. For example, the font commands are under Active Block⇨Font.

Block⇨Copy

Copies a cell or group of selected cells (a block) including the contents and formatting.

For mouse maniacs

The Model Copy button appears only on the Block SpeedBar, but that's OK because that's the SpeedBar you want to use when you are moving or copying things.

Just the facts

When you first select the command, the Block Copy dialog box appears before your very eyes. Why, look! Here's one now.

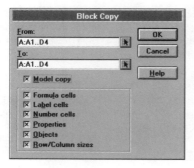

There are two text boxes in the dialog box: From and To. The basics are really quite simple. You put the address of the block you want to copy into the From box and the cell address for the upper-left corner of the new location in the To box, and you click on OK. Faster than waiting in line for the Xerox machine, you have a copy.

Of course, it's always easy to make the process more difficult. One thing that many people try to do is to provide the address for the entire new location. If you do that, be sure that it is the exact same size (same number of rows and columns) as the block you're copying from.

There's also a way to make the process easier. Next to the To and From text boxes are buttons that are called Point Mode buttons. (There's one to the left of this paragraph.) These little buttons appear in most of the Block command dialog boxes. They let you briefly return to the notebook page to select the block with the mouse.

When you click on the Point Mode button, the dialog box is reduced to a floating title bar, and you are returned to the notebook page. You cannot make any changes to the page, but you can use the mouse to select a block. After you have selected the block, double-click on the title bar. If you're not sure what a floating title bar looks like, there's one around here someplace.

Floating title bar

Use the Point Mode button next to the From box to select the From block. Use the one next to the To for the To block.

Putting a check next to the Model Copy option makes the rest of the dialog box available. The remaining items can be used to select what is copied from the block. A check next to an item means that that item will appear in the copy. The Formula cells option controls whether the cells that contain formulas are copied. Similarly, the Label cells option controls whether cells with labels are copied. The Number cells is for cells with just numbers (values). The Properties option controls the copying of all those features that can be set with Active Block, except for row and column sizes (which are handled by the Row/Column sizes option). The final option, Objects, determines whether any objects included in the range are copied.

More stuff

An even better shortcut is available for working with the Point Mode button. Make sure that you start in the text box where you want the address to go. If you can still see the block you want to use on your notebook page behind the dialog box, simply click on a cell in one of the block's corners and hold down the mouse button. The dialog box disappears, and you can drag over the block to select it. When you release the mouse button, the dialog box reappears with the block address inserted. If the block is not showing, you can drag the dialog box to a new location on-screen by clicking on the title bar and holding down the mouse button while moving the dialog box.

You can get the same results by using drag-and-drop editing. Select the block you want to use and then, with the pointer over the selection, hold down the Ctrl key and the left mouse button. When the pointer changes to a grasping hand (called the IRS cursor), simply drag the block outline to its new location and release the mouse button to position the cells. If you don't hold down the Ctrl key, you will move the selection rather than copy it.

When you copy a formula, the addresses are automatically updated for the new location. This is a result of a feature called *relative addressing*. I find this concept easier to understand and explain in terms of people-type relations. Even though we look at the same relation (mother, father, aunt and so on), if we start with different people, we end up with different people.

Here's a simple example: Whether it's good or not, you have a relationship with your mother. She is described as so-and-so's mother, where so-and-so is you. Now, I also have a mother. (Hi, Mom!) She is described as Stuart's mother. Although the relationship is the same — both women are mothers — the person we each are talking about is different because our starting point changes — from you to me. The same thing kinda works with cells. When you copy a formula, the cells that are referenced (or addressed) change because the formula's location has changed.

When I write a formula in cell A3 that refers to A1+A2, Quattro Pro records this formula as "the cell two above plus the cell one above" — kinda like your mother and your mother's mother. When I move the formula to cell B3, Quattro Pro still refers to "the cell two above plus the cell one above," but now the formula refers to cells B1 and B2.

Actually, the common story for why the term *relative address* is used is because when we can talk about things being relative, we mean that two different people may see the same situation very differently, so two different cells can report the same formula very differently. But it's my book, and I like my explanation better.

If you don't want a cell address to change when you copy the formula, put a dollar sign ($) in front of the part you don't want to change. I think of the dollar sign as actually meaning "Don't Change the." So an address written as A1 means "Don't change the *A* and Don't change the *1*." An address like $A1 means "Don't change the *A*, but you can do what you want with the *1*."

Relocate a block of cells by using Block⇨Move. Get rid of a block of cells by using Block⇨Delete. If you want to make several copies of the block, you should use Edit⇨Copy and Edit⇨Paste.

Block⇨Delete

Removes the cells from your spreadsheet. The actual cells are removed so that you have to decide how you want to reorganize what's left. For example, if you delete a row, you usually move the other rows up to take its place. If you delete a block of cells, you can decide whether to fill it in from the left, from below, or from the next page.

For mouse maniacs

The minus sign in the Delete button takes things away. Be careful! It's often better to use Edit⇨Clear or Edit⇨Clear Values.

Just the facts

First thing to do with this command is make sure that it's what you really want. Block⇨Delete actually removes the cells from the spread sheet. You have to rearrange the other cells to fill up the gap. The danger is that using this command can mess up other sections of your spreadsheet. When you're ready to go ahead, it's actually a pretty easy command to use. The Block Delete dialog box is the control center for the command.

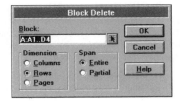

The first thing you have to decide is what it is you want to get rid of and then highlight all the cells to be removed. If you highlight an entire row, an entire column or an entire page, when you select Block⇨Delete, Quattro Pro deletes the entire row, column, or page without bothering you with a dialog box. If you want to delete a partial selection (in other words, a block of cells), select just the block of cells and when you get the Block Delete dialog box, set Span to Partial.

If you are deleting a partial block, your next decision is where Quattro Pro should get the cells to fill the gap you've created. If you set Dimension to Rows, cells from below your block are pulled up to fill the space. If Dimension is set to Columns, cells from the right are moved over to fill in the gap. If you use Pages as the Dimension, cells from all the following pages are moved forward.

After you've decided which cells you are removing and which cells you are moving to fill the gap, you can select OK to actually remove the cells. Check your notebook and make sure that Quattro Pro did exactly what you intended. If not, use Edit⇨Undo to get rid of that attempt and try again.

More stuff

After you delete a block of cells, always check the rest of your notebook before moving on. You may have formulas that are hidden off the screen which have been changed by removing the cells. It's generally safer to delete entire rows or columns. In this way, even if there is a formula that you can't see, the odds are good that you'll delete it, as well.

The two choices in the Span area of the Block Delete dialog box determine whether you delete a block (Partial) or the Entire row, column, or page. For example, even if you only highlight one cell, if you were to select Entire and Pages, the entire page would be removed. To get rid of a block, Span must be set to Partial. You can use these settings to your advantage if you wanted to get rid of an entire column, but you selected only the first few cells by mistake. Simply set Span to Entire and Dimension to Columns. When you click on OK, the entire column vanishes.

When deleting entire rows, columns, or pages, you can avoid the Block Delete dialog box all together. If you have used the borders to make a selection, Block⇨Delete removes the entire selection rather than showing the dialog box. To select a row with the border, click on the row number or drag over the numbers for several rows. To select columns, click on the letter or drag over the letters. To select an entire page, click in the cell where the borders intersect. When you are over the borders, your cursor changes to a big white dot with an arrow or arrows to indicate what dimension you are selecting.

You can use the little button (called the Point Mode button) to the right of the Block text box to select the block on your spreadsheet. When you click on the button, the dialog box is reduced to just a title bar. Select the cells you want from the spreadsheet and then double-click on the dialog box title bar. See the "Just the facts" section of the Block⇨Copy command for a visual example of the Point Mode button.

You can also use the SpeedMenu by first selecting the cell(s) and then clicking the right mouse button (while the pointer is over the selection). You see a nifty pop-up menu, where you can select the Block Delete command.

If you just want to clear out the contents of the cells, use Edit⇨Clear Values. Use Edit⇨Clear to get rid of the formatting as well as the contents.

Block⇨Fill

Calculates a series of values and uses them to fill the selected block. You can enter a series of increasing numbers (such as 1, 2, 3, 4, and so on), a series of decreasing numbers (0, –5, –10, –15, and so on), an exponential and power series, as well as a series of times and dates (such as the dates for the next ten Mondays — Ick!).

Just the facts

The first step is to figure out the pattern for the series you want to create. For most series, you need to know which value the series starts with and how many values there are between items in a series. For example, the series 0, 1, 2, 3 starts with zero and increases by one each time. The series 0, 2, 4, 6 also starts with 0, but it increases by two each time. You can also create series of days of the week, dates, and times as well as more complex mathematical series. After you know how you want to set up your series, select the block and then select the Block⇨Fill command to reveal the Block Fill dialog box.

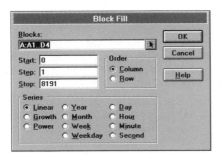

Enter the value that you're using to start the series in the Start box. Put the value that is between items in the series in the Step box. If you want a series such as 0, 2, 4, 6, you would put 0 in the Start box and 2 in the Step box. For a simple series where all the block is in a single row or column and you highlighted all the cells for the block, that's all there is. Select OK and the block will fill with values.

Of course, there's much more to it than this. The most interesting use for fill series is for entering a series of dates. You may notice the Series section at the bottom of the dialog box. If you enter a date as your starting value, you can use the selections in this section to create lists for organizing your information by date. For example, if you enter a date such as Mar-1 and set the series to Month, the block fills with the first day of each of the succeeding months. Even more impressive, if you enter Jan 31 and fill by month, the block fills with the last day of each of the succeeding months — it even knows about leap years.

More stuff

Most of the Series choices are reasonably obvious. The one pair that deserves a bit more explanation is Weekday and Day. If you start with 8/1/94 (a Monday), the first seven days are 8/1, 8/2, 8/3, 8/4, 8/5, 8/6, and 8/7. The first seven weekdays, on the other hand, are 8/1, 8/2, 8/3, 8/4, 8/5, 8/8, and 8/9. The Weekday option skips over any dates that fall on a Saturday or a Sunday.

When working with dates, remember that the format of the value makes a big difference. With a series of dates, you can display them either as 8/1, 8/2, and 8/3 or as Monday, Tuesday, and Wednesday. In general, Quattro Pro uses the same format for the date that you enter for the Start value, but you can always use Active Block⇨Numeric Format to change the look.

If you want a series that runs between two dates — such as a list of the weekdays between August 9 and August 24 — highlight a larger block than you think you'll need and use a Stop value. When you enter a value into the Stop box, Quattro Pro fills the cells until it comes to the end of the block or until it reaches the Stop value, whichever comes first.

There are two other types of numeric series that you can create with Block⇨Fill. Both of them are represented by separate options in the Series section. A Growth series multiplies the preceding item by the Step value. For example, a five-item Growth series starting at 2 with a Step value of 2 results in 2, 4, 8, 16, and 32 (in other words, 2, 2x2, 4x2, 8x2, 16x2). A Power series uses the Step value as an exponent for the preceding item so that a five-item Power series starting at 2 with a Step value of 2 results in 2, 4, 16, 256, and 65,536 (in other words, 2, 2^2, 4^2, 16^2, and 256^2).

Linear, which is the default, adds the St<u>e</u>p value to the preceding item so that the five-item series would be 2, 4, 6, 8, and 10 (in other words, 2, 2+2, 4+2, 6+2, and 8+2).

If your selection is all in a single column or in a single row, you don't need to worry about the setting for Order. If, however, you are filling in a larger block, the Order setting determines which direction is filled in first. Imagine that you're using a block with three rows and three columns and a series that starts at 1 and steps by 1. If Order is set to <u>R</u>ow, the first row contains 1, 2, and 3 with the value 4 placed in the first cell of the second row. If Order is set to <u>C</u>olumn, the first row ends up containing 1, 4, and 7. The 1, 2, and 3 would be down the first column with the 4 in the first cell of the second column.

You can use the little button (called the Point Mode button) to the right of the <u>B</u>locks text box to select the block on your spreadsheet. When you click on the button, the dialog box is reduced to just a title bar. Select the cells you want from the spreadsheet and then double-click on the dialog box title bar. See the "Just the facts" section of the <u>B</u>lock ⇨ <u>C</u>opy command for a visual example of the Point Mode button.

You can also use the SpeedFill command to fill a block with a defined series.

Block ⇨ Insert

Adds a row, column, or block of cells. These are new cells, so the old ones have to be removed to make room. If you add a row, the other rows move down to make room. If you add a block, the other cells can be moved either to the right or down to make the necessary space.

For mouse maniacs

The Block Insert button, with the plus sign, is useful for adding new cells to your spreadsheet.

Just the facts

Most of the time, you'll want to insert an entire row or column into your notebook page. That's easy. For a row, just highlight the row you want to move down (to make room for another row) and select <u>B</u>lock ⇨ <u>I</u>nsert. Bingo! A new row is born. To insert more than one row, just start with the row you want to move down and then highlight as many rows below it as you want to insert. In other words, to enter three rows before row 2, highlight rows 2, 3, and 4.

To insert a new column(s), use the same steps but highlight the column or columns that you want to move to the right. If you need to, you can also insert an entire new page by clicking in the upper-left corner (where your cursor turns to a white dot with two arrows) and then selecting Block⇨Insert.

If you want to get fancy, you can also insert a Partial block. When you insert a block, Quattro Pro has to move the other cells around in order to make room for those that you are adding. How it does this feat is controlled by the options in the Dimension section. If you select Rows, the new cells push the existing cells down on the notebook page. So if I insert new cells in A1 and B1, the information that used to be in A1..B1 would be moved to A2..B2. What was in A2..B2 would be moved to A3..B3 and so on. If you select Columns and insert new cells in A1..B1, the information that was originally in A1..B1 would be moved to C1..D1. The cells from C1..D1 would be in E1..F1 and so on. The final option, Pages, causes the cells to be moved back a page in your notebook. In other words, the cells that were A1..B1 on page A would now be A1..B1 on page B. What was on page B would now be page C and so on.

More stuff

Be careful when inserting a block. If you have formulas that are now showing on-screen, they may be moved by the shifting caused by inserting a block, or the cells that they reference may move. In either case, the shifting may cause the formulas and their values to no longer line up.

You can also use the SpeedMenu by first selecting the cell(s) and then clicking the right mouse button (while the pointer is over the selection). You see a nifty pop-up menu, where you can select the Block Insert command.

After you're in the Block Insert dialog box, you can use the little button (called the Point Mode button) to the right of the Block text box to select the block on your spreadsheet. When you click on the button, the dialog box is reduced to just a title bar. Select the cells you want from the spreadsheet and then double-click on the dialog box title bar. See the "Just the facts" section of the Block⇨Copy command for a visual example of the Point Mode button.

Use the Block⇨Move command to move just the contents of the cells.

Block⇨Move

Takes a cell or group of cells (a block) from one location and plops it down in another. Any formulas contained within the block remain exactly the same. In other words, the addresses for the cells that the formulas use (or *reference*) are not changed.

Just the facts

The Block Move dialog box is one of the most straightforward ones around. It has only two text boxes: From and To. You put the address for the block you want to move into the From box, and you put the address for where you want the block to go into the To box. That's it. When you select OK, Quattro Pro gets a team of movers working on hauling your cells from one place to another. Unlike the movers I used, the Quattro Pro movers move so fast that you can't even see them work.

When you move a block, Quattro Pro makes sure that any formulas that are involved continue to reference the same values, regardless of where you move the formulas or the values. If you move the formula, the addresses (or references) in the formula don't change. On the other hand, if you move a block of values, any formulas that reference those cells change so that they continue to point to the same values. This is the opposite of what happens with the Block⇨Copy command.

More stuff

You can get the same results by using drag-and-drop editing. Select the block you want to use and then, with the pointer over the selection, hold down the left mouse button. When the pointer changes to a grasping hand (called the IRS cursor), simply drag the block outline to its new location and release the mouse button to position the cells. Hold down the Ctrl key when you first press the mouse button to copy the block instead of moving it.

You can use the little button to the right of the To and From text boxes (called the Point Mode button) to select the block on your spreadsheet. When you click on the button, the dialog box is reduced to just a title bar. Select the cells you want from the spreadsheet and then double-click on the dialog box title bar. See the "Just the facts" section of the Block⇨Copy command for a visual example of the Point Mode button.

You have to enter only the cell address for the upper-left corner of the new block in the To box. Be sure to check that the cells you are moving don't write over any information that you want to keep.

There isn't a way to move cells by using relative addresses. Whenever you move a block of cells, the formulas in the block continue to reference the original cells. If you want to move a block and have the formulas change, you have to use two steps: You first copy the block, and you then delete the original.

If you want to duplicate the cell contents, use Block➪Copy. If you want to empty out the cells, use Edit➪Clear. You can also use Edit➪Cut and Edit➪Paste to move the contents of a block of cells.

Block➪Names

Gives a group of cells a name of your choosing. The name makes it easier to write formulas that will make sense several months from now. For example, instead of @Sum(A2..A5)-@Sum(A7..A17), you can write @Sum(Income)-@Sum(Expenses).

For keyboard krazies

$$\boxed{Ctrl} + \boxed{F3}$$

Just the facts

To name a block, simply highlight the cells to be included and select Block➪Names. Enter the name you want to use for the block in the Block Names dialog box and select Add. Or you can open the Block Names dialog box first then select the block by using the Point Mode button next to the Block(s) text box. When you click on the Point Mode button, you are returned to the notebook, where you can highlight your block. Double-click on the Block Names title bar to return to the dialog box.

To remove a single name from the list, highlight the name and then select Delete. To get rid of all the names that you have defined, select Delete All.

The Generate button opens a dialog box for assigning names to blocks that consist of rows or columns of cells with the block name at one end of the block. You highlight a block containing the labels and the cells to be named. The most common example is a series of columns with the block names serving as labels at the top of the column. Your choices for naming columns are Under Top Row (the names are at the top of the column) and Above Bottom Row (the names are at the bottom of the column). The choices for naming rows are Right of Leftmost Column (the names are to the far left) and Left of Rightmost Column (the names are to the far right). In the figure, selecting Under Top Row gives each column a color name, and selecting Right of Leftmost Column gives each row a flower name. Note that you can use more than one of these options for a single row.

When you choose the final option, Name Cells at Intersection, each cell in the grid is given a name that uses a combination of the label for the row and the label for the column. In the example in the figure, each cell would have two names — the flower name followed by the color and the color followed by the flower name. The two parts of the name are separated by an underscore (_).

The Labels button performs a similar task to that of the Generate button. The Labels button automatically names a bunch of cells at once. With Generate, however, you highlight both the names and the cells to be named. With Labels, you highlight only the cells containing the names, and you name only a single cell. You then have to tell Quattro Pro whether the cell to be named is to the Right of the label, to the Left of the label, Up above the label, or Down below the label.

In the example I just used, I could name the cells in the second column by highlighting the flower names, opening the Block Names dialog box and then selecting Labels. I would then select Right in the Create Names From Labels dialog box and, finally, select OK. Each cell in the second column next to the flower names would now have a name. For example, cell B2 would be named Roses (because B2 is the cell to the right of the label Roses). The cells in the other columns would not be named.

The Output button is used to create a list of all the labels in your notebook. You probably want to go to a new page before using this option. Selecting the Output button opens the Name Table dialog box. To use the Name Table dialog box, just select a block that is two cells wide in the row where you want the table to start. Quattro Pro will use as many rows as necessary to list all the names in the table.

More stuff

If you design notebooks for other people or that you don't use often but you depend upon, it is a very good idea to get in the habit of using names. The additional work of creating the names is more than balanced by the fact that when you look at your formulas six months from now, you'll actually have some idea of what they do.

You can also use the SpeedMenu by first selecting the cell(s) and then clicking the right mouse button (while the pointer is over the selection). You see a nifty pop-up menu, where you can select the Names command.

If you move or delete either of the *corner cells* of a named block, all references to that block will be lost, and any formulas using that block will display ERR. The corner cells are the cells named in the block definition. For the block Q12..T15, the corner cells are Q12 and T15. You can change the contents of the cells without affecting the names.

You can also assign a name to a group of blocks. To highlight more than one block, highlight your first block normally and then hold down the Ctrl key as you highlight the other blocks in the group.

Use Active Page⇨Name to give the entire page its own name. For information on using the Point Mode button, see Block⇨Copy.

Block⇨Reformat

Adjusts very long labels so that they fit in the selected cells. If you highlight a group of cells in the same row, this command pushes the text into as many rows as needed. If you highlight a block with cells in two or more rows, Quattro Pro fits as much as the text as possible into your selected cells. If the text doesn't fit in the selected block, you get a very nice message telling you to try again.

Just the facts

There are two ways to use this command. The first method forces the text in the first cell to be broken into as many rows as necessary to fit within the selected columns. You need to highlight the cell containing the text and as many columns in the same row as you want to use for the information. Select Block⇨Reformat and then select OK. The text is broken into individual lines that use as many rows as necessary. Each line of text is placed in a cell in the first selected column.

Imagine that you have a long title in cell A1. You want it broken into several rows in columns A and B. Highlight cells A1 and B1, select Block⇨Reformat, and then click on OK. The text is broken into several lines, none of which extend into column C. A sentence such as "The rain in Spain stays mainly on the plain" could be broken into as many as three lines. The phrase "The rain in Spain" would be in cell A1; the phrase "stays mainly on" would be in cell A2; and "the plain" would be in cell A3.

The second method is to highlight the entire block that you want filled with the text. If you highlight cells in more than one row, Quattro Pro tries to reformat the text to fit within the block. If it can't reformat the text, you see the following message: `Not enough room in reformat block`. At this point, you have three choices: You can highlight a bigger block, change the column widths to make the block larger, or edit the text so that it's smaller.

More stuff

Any cell in the block you have selected that contains text — other than the first one — is treated as though it were empty. Quattro Pro assumes that the text in the first column can overlap into the next columns. If one of the other cells contains text, the existing text is displayed instead of the reformatted text. If your reformatted text is in cells A1, A2, and A3 and extends over three columns, any text that is in B2 would be shown instead of the overlapping text from A2.

You can use the little button (called the Point Mode button) to the right of the Block text to select the block on your spreadsheet. When you click on the button, the dialog box is reduced to just a title bar. Select the cells you want from the spreadsheet and then double-click on the dialog box title bar. See the "Just the facts" section of the Block▷Copy command for a visual example of the Point Mode button.

You use Active Block▷Alignment to control whether cells have word wrap active. The other command for breaking words into different cells is Notebook▷Parse. To automatically format a block of cells with borders, shading, and font changes, you need to use SpeedFormat.

Block▷Restrict Input

Prevents the use of any menu, SpeedBar, or Property Band commands. You use this command when you are designing a worksheet and want to prevent anyone from even trying to enter something into the protected cells.

Just the facts

In order to restrict input, you must first unprotect some of your cells by using Active Block▷Constraints. Generally, you unprotect the cells that will contain values to be used in the formulas and protect everything else. Next, highlight a block containing all the unprotected cells and select Block▷Restrict Input. If you select your block first, the only thing you need to do in the dialog box is select OK. Otherwise, use the Point Mode button to go back to your notebook and select your block before selecting OK.

When you return to your notebook, you'll discover that the menu bar is gray and that you cannot use any of the buttons on the SpeedBar or any of the lists on the Property Band — all they do is beep at you. You can move between unprotected cells and enter information. The advantage is that your movement keys now jump you from one unprotected cell to another and skip over any protected cells that fall in between. This command makes entering data much easier.

More stuff

Although restricting the cells for input makes the notebook a bit easier to use, it doesn't really offer any security. To go back to using the menus normally, all you have to do is press Escape.

You can use the little button box (called the Point Mode button) to the right of the Input Block text box to select the block on your spreadsheet. When you click on the button, the dialog box is reduced to just a title bar. Select the cells you want from the spreadsheet and then double-click on the dialog box title bar. See the "Just the facts" section of the Block⇨Copy command for a visual example of the Point Mode button.

Prepare a range of cells by making them unprotected with the Active Block⇨Constraints command. Turn on cell protection by using Active Page⇨Protection.

Block⇨Sort

Puts things in order. You can use the Sort Block dialog box to sort a block of cells that uses up to five columns within the block as your sort keys. You can use the SpeedBar buttons to sort a block based upon the first column.

For mouse maniacs

The top half of the SpeedSort button uses the left column to sort the block into ascending order.

The bottom half of the SpeedSort button uses the left column to sort the block into descending order.

Just the facts

When you use the SpeedBar buttons, there are only two steps to worry about. First, highlight the block of cells that you want to sort and make sure that the column you intend to use for sorting is the leftmost column. The second and final step is to click on either the top half of the SpeedSort button (the up arrow) to sort into ascending order or the bottom half (the down arrow) to sort into descending order. There is no way to use the SpeedSort button to sort on multiple columns or on any column other than the leftmost.

If you want greater control over your sort, you need to use the Block⇨Sort command and the resulting Block Sort dialog box.

Although the Block Sort dialog box is a bit intimidating at first glance, it's really not that hard to use. The Block section tells Quattro Pro which block to sort. If you highlight a block before you select the command, its address is already inserted into the box. The Reset button is used to clear all the boxes (including the Block box) and reset the options back to their defaults.

Two option pairs control how Quattro Pro sorts your information. In the Data pair, you must decide whether to put the Numbers first or the Labels first when sorting in ascending order. Because numbers and labels are sorted differently, you have to decide which group comes first. (See the first note in "More stuff.") The other pair of choices controls what Quattro Pro does with the difference between uppercase and lowercase letters. With Character Code, all of the uppercase letters are sorted together, and then the lowercase letters are sorted (when sorting in ascending order). In other words, after sorting, your order would be Apple, Banana, Cherry, artichoke, bean, carrot. With Dictionary sorting, the case of the letters is ignored, so you'd get Apple, artichoke, Banana, bean, carrot, Cherry.

The last, but certainly not the least, section is Sort Keys. In this section, you actually give Quattro Pro its marching orders. A Sort Key is a column that Quattro Pro uses to sort the information. When you are using the Sort Block dialog box, the key can be any column within the selected block. (With the SpeedSort buttons, you can use only the leftmost column as your single key.) Notice that there are five boxes for keys marked as the 1st through the 5th. You use these boxes to indicate the key columns. (The concept of Sort Keys is explained under "More stuff.")

To use the Sort Keys within Quattro Pro, simply enter the address for any cell or block containing the information for your first key in the 1st box. Then decide whether you want the information sorted in ascending order or not. If you clear the Ascending check box, the information is sorted in Descending order. If you are going to use more than one key, enter the other keys in the 2nd through 5th boxes. When you select OK, Quattro Pro reorganizes the selected rows based on your instructions in the dialog box.

More stuff

With more than one Sort Key, each level of keys is used within the preceding level, which means that Quattro Pro sorts your information on the 1st key and then looks to see if there are any rows where the 1st key was the same. If Quattro Pro finds any, it looks to the column you have marked as the 2nd key and uses it to sort only those rows with matching 1st keys. Although this may sound confusing, you are already accustomed to this kind of sort. When you look at a phone book, for example, the first key is the last name, and the second key is the first name. Only when you have more than one family with the same last name (such as Smith) does the first name matter. The third key, the middle name or initial, is hardly used at all, but there is a fourth key (for names that match exactly or for people who only list their last name). The fourth key is address.

One odd thing about how the Order options work: The word *first* applies only to sorts in Ascending order. If you sort in Descending order and select Numbers first, the numbers appear after the labels.

The difference between sorting numbers and labels applies mostly to how Quattro Pro handles cells that contain digits. The series 1, 2, 11, 25, 200 is sorted as numbers. In other words, the items have been put in order based upon their values. If you were to sort the same series as labels, the order would be 1, 11, 2, 200, 21. Pretty strange, huh? Well, not if you think of the items as words. When Quattro Pro sorts labels, it looks at the items character by character. Just like it puts all the words that start with *A* before any of the words that start with *B*, it puts all the items that start with *1* before any of those that start with *2*. It then looks at the second character and puts any spaces before other values and puts the item with a *0* before the one with a *5*. If you have a block that contains some numbers as numbers and some as labels, you will have trouble sorting them until you make them all the same (either all numbers or all labels).

You can use the little button (called the Point Mode button) to the right of the Block and Sort Keys text boxes to select the block on your spreadsheet. When you click on the button, the dialog box is reduced to just a title bar. Select the cells you want from the spreadsheet and then double-click on the dialog box title bar. See the "Just the facts" section of the Block⇨Copy command for a visual example of the Point Mode button.

The secrets of organizing the universe (or at least your data) are covered in Chapter 10 of *Quattro Pro 6 For Windows For Dummies*.

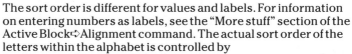

The sort order is different for values and labels. For information on entering numbers as labels, see the "More stuff" section of the Active Block⇨Alignment command. The actual sort order of the letters within the alphabet is controlled by Application⇨Language. For information about entering numbers as labels, see the "More stuff" section of the Application⇨Align command.

Block⇨Transpose

Switches rows for columns or vice versa. If you transpose a block that is two columns wide and five columns tall, you end up with a new block that is five columns wide and two columns tall.

For mouse maniacs

The icon on the Transpose button (from the Block SpeedBar) makes it clear what happens when you transpose a block.

Just the facts

One of the most common uses of the Block⇨Transpose command is for moving the row of labels that runs across the top of your worksheet so that it runs down the first column. The second most common use is turning the leftmost column into the first row. To do either of these tasks, simply put the block address of the information you want to move in the From box and put the address of where you want the information to go in the To box. (As with most commands, you can just enter the cell address for the upper-left corner of the block in the To box.)

Suppose that you have labels in the first row in cells B1..F1 that you want in the first column. Highlight the block, select Block⇨Transpose, make sure that you are in the To box, select A2, and then click on OK. The labels are now in both B1..F1 and in A2..A6. You now probably want to get rid of the set in B1..F1.

More stuff

If you want to switch two sets of labels, you need to transpose one into another area of the worksheet, transpose the second set into the spot where the first set started, and then finally move the transposed first set to where the second set started from.

Highlighting a square block and flipping it end-for-end in the same location should work with the Transpose command, but it doesn't. What you actually get is fairly unpredictable. To make it work, place the transposed block in a new location.

You can use the little button (called the Point Mode button) to the right of the To and From text boxes to select the block on your spreadsheet. When you click on the button, the dialog box is reduced to just a title bar. Select the cells you want from the spreadsheet and then double-click on the dialog box title bar. See the "Just the facts" section of the Block⇨Copy command for a visual example of the Point Mode button.

To read about this command in action, see Chapter 10 in *Quattro Pro 6 For Windows For Dummies*.

If you want to move a only a block, use <u>B</u>lock⇨<u>M</u>ove.

Block⇨Values

Converts formulas into their values. You can either replace the values in their current location or make a copy of the values in another location. Although using this command speeds up recalculations in your worksheet, it also means that those values will never change again. You should only convert formulas after you are sure the values that you are using are final.

For mouse maniacs

The Block SpeedBar contains the Values button for converting the formulas in the selected cells into values.

Just the facts

This command is one of the easiest to use. First, highlight the block containing the formulas you want to convert into values. Next, select <u>B</u>lock⇨<u>V</u>alues. Finally, select OK, and those pesky formulas are gone.

More stuff

If you want to make a copy of the block that contains values instead of formulas, you simply need to place the location for the values in the <u>T</u>o box before selecting OK in the Block Values dialog box.

You can get a similar result by using <u>E</u>dit⇨Paste Spec<u>i</u>al. For more elaborate transformations, see <u>T</u>ools⇨<u>C</u>onsolidator.

Edit⇨Clear

Empties the cell. Everything associated with the cell is removed, including the contents, the formatting, and any properties.

For mouse maniacs

 The Clear button on the Block SpeedBar totally wipes out the cell.

Just the facts

Select a block and then select Edit⇨Clear to remove all the information from the cell, including any formatting and property information. That's all there is to it.

More stuff

The difference between Edit⇨Clear Values and Edit⇨Clear is that Clear Values leaves the formatting and any other settings from the Active Block properties. Clear removes everything.

 You can also use the SpeedMenu by first selecting the cell(s) and then clicking the right mouse button (while the pointer is over the selection). You see a nifty pop-up menu, where you can select the Clear command.

If you just want to clear out the contents of the cell (values or labels), use Edit⇨Clear Values. If you want to be able to put the contents somewhere else, you should use Edit⇨Cut (or just use Block⇨Move to get them to the new location in one step). If you want to get rid of the physical cells, use Block⇨Delete.

Edit⇨Clear Values

Gets rid of the contents in whatever cells are selected. This command can be problematic if you confuse it with Edit⇨Cut. Cut lets you move your information to another location, but Clear Values destroys your information.

For mouse maniacs

 This is the kinder, gentler button available on the Block SpeedBar.

For keyboard krazies

Just the facts

This command is (unfortunately) one of the easiest commands to use. Just highlight what you want to get rid of and press the Delete key. It's a real bummer to have something highlighted, reach for another key, and hit Delete by mistake. If this happens to you, use Edit⇨Undo right away.

More stuff

The difference between Edit⇨Clear Values and Edit⇨Clear is that Clear Values leaves the formatting and any other settings from the Active Block properties. Clear removes everything. Edit⇨Clear is one step short of Block⇨Delete, which actually removes the cells themselves.

You can also use the SpeedMenu by first selecting the cell(s) and then clicking the right mouse button (while the pointer is over the selection). You see a nifty pop-up menu, where you can select the Clear Value(s) command. Clear Value(s) on the pop-up menu is the same as Clear Values on the Edit menu.

To clear out the formatting as well as the contents, use Edit⇨Clear. If you want to move highlighted information somewhere else, you should use Edit⇨Cut or Block⇨Move.

Edit⇨Copy

Makes a copy of whatever you have selected and puts it onto the Clipboard (a super-secret nerd place). You use this command (with Edit⇨Paste) for making more than one copy of existing information. Otherwise, you can just use Block⇨Copy.

For mouse maniacs

The Copy button is one of my favorites — just be sure that you have something highlighted first. You can do anything you want before pasting except use Edit⇨Cut or another Edit⇨Copy command.

For keyboard krazies

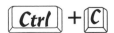

Just the facts

There are basically four steps (and two commands) involved in using Edit⇨Copy. The first step is to highlight the information you want to make a copy of. Second, select Edit⇨Copy. This action puts a copy of whatever you had highlighted onto the Clipboard. The third step is to move to the place where you want the new copy of the information. You can use any of the methods that you know for moving, none of which will change what's on the Clipboard. The fourth and final step is to actually insert the information from the Clipboard by selecting Edit⇨Paste. That's all there is to it.

If you want to put the information in more than one spot, simply move to another location and select Edit⇨Paste again. You can paste as many times as you want to make your copies. Notice that only one thing can be on the Clipboard at a time. If you copy (or cut) something new, the old information is thrown out.

More stuff

You can also use the SpeedMenu by first selecting the cell(s) and then clicking the right mouse button (while the pointer is over the selection). You see a nifty pop-up menu, where you can select the Copy command.

If you want to replace some old information with what you have just copied, highlight the old information before pasting.

You can also use the Cut, Copy and Paste commands from the Edit menu to edit the text within a cell. For example, if you want to copy only part of a cell's contents, open the cell for editing by double-clicking on it or by pressing F2. Then highlight the portion of the text you want to copy. Press Return to close the input line. Next, go to the cell where you want to paste the information. If you want to replace all the cell's contents, select Edit⇨Paste. If you want to insert it into the text already in the cell, open the input line (by double-clicking the cell or by pressing F2) and then move to where you want to insert. Now, when you select Edit⇨Paste the text will be inserted at the cursor's location.

The Cut, Copy and Paste commands from the Edit menu can also be used to move information between programs. With these commands, you move information in and out of your notebook. If you copy something into your notebook, the copy is formatted by Quattro Pro and is totally independent of the original program. In fact, you can throw the original away or change it completely. In contrast, with the Edit⇨Insert Object or File⇨Subscribe commands, Quattro Pro and the other program remain in touch with each other, which means that any changes in the original are automatically included in your database.

For another perspective on the joys of Cut, Copy, and Paste, see Chapter 10 in *Quattro Pro 6 For Windows For Dummies.*

You can copy a block of cells in a single step by using Block⇨Copy. If you want to move the information, you can use a combination of Edit⇨Cut and Edit⇨Paste or use Block⇨Move. If you want to copy only the properties, you can use Edit⇨Copy along with Edit⇨Paste Special.

Edit⇨Cut

Takes whatever you have selected and puts it onto the Clipboard (a super-secret nerd place). You use this command (along with Edit⇨Paste) to move information, or you can use Block⇨Move to move the information in a single step.

For mouse maniacs

Dig those little scissors. You may notice that they're a lot bigger than Microsoft's.

For keyboard krazies

[*Ctrl*] + [X]

Just the facts

There are basically four steps (and two commands) involved in using Edit⇨Cut. The first step is to let Quattro Pro know what information you want to work with by highlighting what you want to move. Next, select Edit⇨Cut. What you had highlighted disappears and is stored on the Clipboard. You then need to move to where you want to put the information. You can use any of the methods that you know for moving because none of them will change what's on the Clipboard. You can move around on the same page, to another page in the same notebook, or to another notebook. To actually insert the information, select Edit⇨Paste. That's all there is to it. The information is gone from its old position and inserted where you now want it. Remember that only one thing can be on the Clipboard at a time. If you copy (or cut) something new, the old information on the Clipboard is thrown out.

Just like with the Edit⇨Copy command, you can put the information in more than one spot. Simply move to another location and select Edit⇨Paste again. You can paste as many times as you want to make your new copies. Also, if you want to replace some old information with what you have just copied, highlight the old information before selecting Edit⇨Paste.

More stuff

You can also use the Cut command from the SpeedMenu by first selecting the cell(s) and then clicking the right mouse button (while the pointer is over the selection). You see a nifty pop-up menu, where you can select the Cut command.

You can also use the Cut, Copy and Paste commands to edit the text within a cell. For example, if you want to copy only part of a cell's contents, open the cell for editing by double-clicking on the cell or by pressing F2. Then highlight the portion of the text you want to copy. Press Return to close the input line. Next, go to the cell where you want to paste the information. If you want to replace all the cell's contents, select Edit⇨Paste. If you want to insert it into the text already in the cell, open the input line (by double-clicking on the cell or by pressing F2) and then move to where you want to insert. Now, when you select Edit⇨Paste, the text will be inserted at the cursor's location.

For another perspective on the joys of Cut, Copy, and Paste, see Chapter 10 in *Quattro Pro 6 For Windows For Dummies*.

To move information in a single step, use Block⇨Move. If you want to duplicate the information, use Edit⇨Copy and Edit⇨Paste, or just Block⇨Copy. If you're trying to replace formulas with their values, use Block⇨Values.

Edit⇨Find and Replace

Lets you track down information in your worksheet and change it. You can also use this command to convert formulas that match what you're looking for into values.

Just the facts

This command is one of two where the wonderful world of word processing meets that of spreadsheets. (The other is Tools⇨Spell Check.) To use the command, you need to decide three things: where you want to change things, what things you want to change, and what you're changing them into. If you want to simply search for something, you need only the first two.

In the Find/Replace dialog box, put the address of the block that you want searched in the Block(s) text box, the information about what you're looking for in the Find box, and the information about what you're going to change it into in the Replace box. You then can click on the Replace All button to change every occurrence of the text in the Find box with whatever is in the Replace box. If you've put numbers into the Find box, Quattro Pro looks within the actual formulas for matches.

If you just want to search for something, don't worry about what's in the Replace box. Simply click on the Find Next button to move to the first cell containing whatever is in the Find box. If you want to search backward through the block (or if you found what you were looking for and went past it), you can click on the Previous button.

If you want to replace some but not all of the matches for what is in the Find box, you can use the Find Next button to move to the first example and then decide whether to replace it (by clicking on the Replace button) or to skip over it (by clicking on the Find Next button).

The Options section lets you have greater control over the search. Unless told otherwise, Quattro Pro starts searching in the upper-left cell and works its way across the first row in the block before moving on to the next row. If you put a check next to Columns First, Quattro Pro still starts in the upper-left corner but moves down the first column before starting the next.

Use the Match Whole option to instruct Quattro Pro to ignore text that matches what is in the Find box if it is contained within another word. For example, Quattro Pro normally matches the *mess* in *message*. With Match Whole checked, Quattro Pro ignores the match contained in another word.

The Case Sensitive option, when checked, requires that the upper- and lower-case letters in the text match exactly. With this option cleared, Quattro Pro matches *apple* with *apple*, *Apple*, or *APPLE*. With the option checked, *apple* matches only with *apple*.

The other two words would be skipped.

Over in the Look In box are two buttons which control whether Quattro Pro looks for matches within the formula (the default setting) or looks just at the results of the formula. If you select For_mula and have a 2 in the _Find box and a 3 in the R_eplace box, Quattro Pro leaves the formula +1+1 alone but changes +1+2 to read +1+3. With _Value selected and the same text in the _Find and R_eplace boxes, Quattro Pro replaces +1+1 with a 3 and leaves +1+2 alone.

The third choice in the Look In box, Con_dition, does something a little different. Instead of looking for a match for the text in the _Find box, it uses the text as a test for searching. For example, putting ?>5 in the _Find box and selecting Con_dition and _Value tells Quattro Pro to search for any cell that is displaying a value greater than 5. You can include text in the R_eplace box and have the contents of every matching cell changed to the R_eplace text. If you want to ignore some of the cells in the block when searching for a Con_dition, simply include the first cells to be searched in the _Find text. For example, B7>5 says ignore any cells before B7 and then start looking for ones with values greater than five. Remember that the C_olumns First option determines what order Quattro Pro considers the cells to be in.

Use the _Close button to exit the dialog box and the Re_set button to clear out all the information and start with a bland dialog box.

More stuff

If you leave the _Block(s) box blank (say that fast three times), Quattro Pro searches the current page, starting with cell A1.

You can learn all about sending Quattro Pro on seek and destroy missions with the _Find and Replace command in Chapter 10 in *Quattro Pro 6 For Windows For Dummies*.

If you want to replace all the formulas in the selection with their values, use _Block⇨_Values. If you want to go to a specific cell, specific page, or named location, you can use _Edit⇨_Go to.

Edit⇨Go to

Takes you where you want to go within the active notebook. This command can save you the time it takes to flip through pages while you look for a particular location. If you used names, you can go directly to a named block.

For mouse maniacs

⏩   The Fast Page Forward button (to the right of the scroll bar at the bottom of the screen) shows you the next screenful of pages (with one overlapping column).

▶   The Page Forward button (down by the horizontal scroll bar) takes you to the preceding page.

◀   The Page Back button (also down at the bottom of the screen) takes you to the next page.

⏪   The Fast Page Back button jumps you to the preceding screen's worth of pages (with one overlapping column).

⊞   When you are working with tables (a block of cells surrounded by empty cells), the Top Left of Table button on the Modeling SpeedBar moves you to the upper-left corner of the current block.

⊞   The Top Right of Table button on the Modeling SpeedBar, not too surprisingly, takes you to the cell in the upper-right corner of the table.

⊞   To get to the lower-left corner of the table, click on the Bottom Left of Table button on the Modeling SpeedBar.

⊞   The Bottom Right of Table button is also on the Modeling SpeedBar and jumps you to the lower-right corner of the table.

For keyboard krazies

Just the facts

The buttons described in the "For mouse maniacs" section don't actually use the Go to dialog box, but they do move you around in the notebook. To use the dialog box, either select the Edit⟶Go to command or press F5.

If you know the address of the cell you want to visit, just type it in the Reference box of the Go to dialog box and select OK. There you are. You've moved to the cell you described. You can optionally include a page reference as part of the cell address.

You can also move to named blocks or other pages. In the dialog box, you are given a list of all named blocks (see Block⟶Names for how to assign names) and a list of all the pages. The list of named blocks is alphabetized while the list of pages is in the order they appear. You can either enter a name in the Reference box (by typing it or highlighting it from one of the lists) or immediately jump to that location by double-clicking on the name in the list.

More stuff

When working with the Block Names or Pages lists in the Go to dialog box, you can click once in either list and type the first letter of a name to jump to the first name that starts with that letter. Press the letter again to move to the next name starting with that letter.

For a list of all the nifty techniques for moving around within your worksheet, see Chapter 3 in *Quattro Pro 6 For Windows For Dummies*.

If you're not sure where you want to go, you can use Edit⇨Find and Replace. If you want to go to the Objects Page, use View⇨Objects Page.

Edit⇨Insert Break

Inserts a row with a page break marker in the first cell. The page break is created by two colons (forming the corners of a square) and must appear within a cell by itself. To get rid of the page break, just delete the code.

Just the facts

In general, you can simply select the row where you want the new page to start and then select Edit⇨Insert Break. The only time this technique doesn't work is if you are going to print a block of cells. In this case, the page break must be in the first column of the block (which is not necessarily in column A). You highlight the cell that you want to start the new page and select the command.

More stuff

Anything else contained in the row with the page break symbol will not print; therefore, you can use this row for notes to yourself (or the person using the notebook) that will appear on-screen but not on the printed page.

You can control the page breaks created by the margins by using File⇨Page Setup.

Edit⇨Insert Object

Creates an OLE relationship with a document, or *object*, created by another program. One of the coolest uses for this command allows you to include pictures and sound within your worksheet. I haven't seen very many practical uses for it, however.

Just the facts

Although not as dangerous as bullfighting, OLE is part of the very newest Windows technology (and is, therefore, more likely to break). However, because you paid your money, I'll give you a quick overview of inserting objects, but bear in mind that OLE is pretty nerdy stuff.

Basically, Insert Object lets you add in something created in another program. If you link to the object, the object exists as a file on disk. If you embed the object, it is included as part of your database. You can display the object either as it would be seen in the other program or as an icon. Whether you are linking or embedding an object or whether you intend to show it as an object or an icon, you must first go to where you want the object to appear and then select Edit⇨Insert Object. You get the Insert Object dialog box:

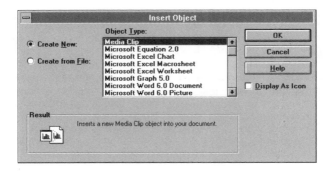

Talk about your involved dialog boxes! The contents of this one changes based on what you have installed on your computer, but the process is fairly straightforward after you decide what type of object you want.

To use an object that already exists as a file on your system, click on the Create From File button. The Object Type list disappears to be replaced with a File text box. If you know the filename, by all means type it in. Otherwise, you can click on the Browse button to open a dialog box to find the file containing the object. After you've found the file, double-click on it (or highlight it and press Enter) to return to the dialog box.

You now have to make a choice. If you want to embed an independent copy of the object, make sure that the Link box is cleared. If you want to link to the original files so that any changes are carried into Quattro Pro, make sure that the Link box is checked. The good news is that Quattro Pro should be able to figure out what type of object you are trying to insert.

To create a new object that exists only within your spreadsheet, select the Create New option and then select what type of object you want in the Object Type list. Highlight the object type (based on the program that will create it, such as a Media Clip) and click on OK (or press Enter). You're now in the other program that will create the object. Do whatever you need to create the object (after buying the appropriate . . . *For Dummies* book and its accompanying *Quick Reference*) and then select the last command, probably Exit, on the File menu. You are returned to Quattro Pro. That's it. The object has been inserted.

More stuff

There's another decision that you have to make along the way: whether to display the actual object or an icon representing the object. The Display As Icon check box can be very useful when you are inserting certain types of objects. For example, some objects (such as sounds) have to be displayed as icons. Furthermore, with many types of objects, using icons lets your system work faster because it doesn't have to draw a complex picture each time you switch records. Finally, there is an additional advantage when formatting your pages because the icons are all the same size.

The Object Type list can include programs that you once had but have now deleted (or at least temporarily removed from your system). The problem is that the available objects are registered when a program is added and there isn't a standard way to remove them. Just restrict your choices to the programs you know are on your machine.

Because OLE is a Microsoft standard, Novell would probably prefer that you use the Object Exchange (OBEX) to include information with the File⇨Subscribe command. If you just want to import the contents of a file, you don't have to worry about all this nerdy stuff, and you can use one of the following commands: Notebook⇨Extract, Notebook⇨Insert, or Notebook⇨Text Import.

Edit⇨Paste

Inserts whatever is currently on the Clipboard. You put things onto the Clipboard by using either the Edit⇨Cut or the Edit⇨Copy command. You can keep selecting Edit⇨Paste to insert multiple copies.

For mouse maniacs

 One click of the Paste button inserts whatever you cut or copied last. The button is available only when you are working with datasheets.

For keyboard krazies

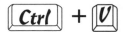

Just the facts

In order for this command to do any good, you must have put something onto the Clipboard by using either Edit⇨Copy or Edit⇨Cut. The Edit⇨Paste command takes the content of the Clipboard and inserts it at the cursor. You can paste the same thing into different locations as many times as you want.

You have two choices when pasting a block. You can either select the upper-left corner of the area where you want to put the block or you can select a block the exact size of the one on the Clipboard. The first approach is easier. The second approach makes sure that you realize what information you are pasting over.

More stuff

You can also use the Cut, Copy and Paste commands to edit the text within a cell. For example, if you want to copy only part of a cell's contents, open the cell for editing by double-clicking on the cell or by pressing F2. Then highlight the portion of the text you want to copy. Press Return to close the input line. Next, go to the cell where you want to paste the information. If you want to replace all the cell's contents, select Edit⇨Paste. If you want to insert the new information into the text already in the cell, open the input line (by double-clicking on the cell or by pressing F2) and then move to where you want to insert. Now when you select Edit⇨Paste, the text is inserted at the cursor's location.

If you have anything selected, Edit⇨Paste replaces that information with whatever is in the Clipboard.

You can also use the SpeedMenu by first selecting the cell(s) and then clicking the right mouse button (while the pointer is over the selection). You see a nifty pop-up menu, where you can select the Paste command.

For another perspective on the joys of Cut, Copy and Paste, see Chapter 10 in *Quattro Pro 6 For Windows For Dummies*.

Of course Edit⇨Paste works only if you put something on the Clipboard with Edit⇨Cut or Edit⇨Copy. If you want greater control over what portions of the block you are pasting, you should use Edit⇨Paste Special.

Edit⇨Paste Special

Copies formats and properties from one block to another, creates a copy of a block with values instead of formulas, creates links between pages or notebooks, and makes a transposed copy. In other words, you use this command when you want to do something fancy with the contents of the Clipboard.

For mouse maniacs

 The Paste Properties button on the Format SpeedBar pastes only the properties of the block on the Clipboard.

 The Paste Link button on the Block SpeedBar lets you create a link back to the source of the Clipboard's contents.

Just the facts

This is the Dr. Jekyll/Mr. Hyde command. The dialog box that you get can be different, depending on what's on the Clipboard. You get either a dialog box for controlling how Quattro Pro inserts a block or a dialog box for creating an OLE object.

When pasting information that you get from within Quattro Pro, you get this Paste Special dialog box.

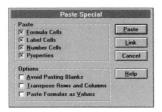

Your first decision is what to paste. Your choices are Formula Cells, Label Cells, Number Cells, Properties, or some combination of these. Putting a check next to any of the first three items (which reference the types of cells) tells Quattro Pro to paste any cells of that type from the Clipboard. Leaving these check boxes blank means that cells of this type are not pasted. For example, to paste the labels and values from a block without the formulas, you would clear the check from Formula Cells and leave the other two checked.

The fourth option, Properties, controls whether features (including formatting) set with the Active Block command are pasted. With this option checked, the formatting from the block on the Clipboard is pasted onto the cells. You can use this by clearing the first three options and just pasting the format. Conversely, you can check the first three options and leave Properties cleared in order to use the formats that have already been given to the cells where you are pasting the information.

The choices in the Options section give you access to a number of features that duplicate commands on the Block menu. You can check Transpose Rows and Columns to get an effect similar to that of Block⇨Transpose — your first row becomes the first column; the second row becomes the second column; and so on. Checking Paste Formulas as Values gives an effect similar to that of Block⇨Values — formulas are replaced with their results.

The Avoid Pasting Blanks option ignores any blank cells on the Clipboard. Rather than including the blanks in the newly pasted block (and replacing whatever used to be in those cells), the cells are not pasted (so the old information remains).

You can use the Link button on the Paste Special dialog box to create a *hotlink*, which is similar to an OLE object link. The only restriction is that you have to be pasting in a different location from where you copied the original. Any changes in the original block are also made to the linked block. (Actually, all Quattro Pro does is insert a series of formulas that reference back to the original block.)

If the content of the Clipboard is from another program, Paste Special creates an OLE object by using this version of the Paste Special dialog box.

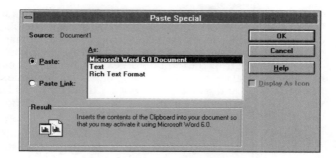

An OLE object is only "sorta" inserted into your notebook. You need the original program that created the object in order to make any changes. The first step is to put the information (whether its a picture, sounds, or whatever) onto the Clipboard. You do this by using the Edit⇨Copy command in the program where you created the stuff. (You can use Edit⇨Cut, but it's generally better to leave the original and make a copy instead.)

After you choose the location within your notebook for the new information, simply select Edit⇨Paste Special and then click on the Link button. You then pick the type of object that you're working with from the list. In most cases, Quattro Pro will have guessed correctly, and you can just click OK.

More stuff

There's actually a third type of Paste Special dialog box that is available when you have cut or copied information from a graph. This dialog box is used to apply attributes from one graph to another. The choices include graph type, position, titles, data series, background, color scheme, annotations, or any combination.

You can also use Paste Special to convert information from another program that is on the Clipboard into a different format. In general, there is no point in making such a change, but sometimes a different format provides better performance or makes graphics appear crisper. To use a different format, simply click on the Paste button and select the new format from the list.

With OLE objects, you also need to decide whether to display the actual object or an icon representing the object. Check the Display As Icon check box when you want to display an icon rather than the entire object in the new location. Use an icon to represent such objects as sounds, to speed up your system, or to make formatting your pages easier (because icons are all the same size).

If you need to replace formulas with their values, use Block⇨Values. Use Block⇨Transpose to change the orientation of the block. Selectively copying aspects of a block can also be handled by Block⇨Copy. If the information that you want to paste is already stored in a file, you can use Edit⇨Insert Object instead (and you don't have to bother with the Clipboard).

Edit⇨Select All

Selects the entire worksheet in a single step.

For mouse maniacs

You can select the entire table by clicking the spot where the row numbers and column letters intersect.

If you're working with the Modeling SpeedBar, you can use the Select Entire Table button, which selects a block of cells surrounded by white space.

Just the facts

This command is what one of my friends calls a "no brainer." (Hi Devra.) You select the command, and it does exactly what you expect it to do. Select Edit⇨Select All, and the entire page is selected.

More stuff

To select an entire row, simply click on the row number at the far left. To select several rows, drag over the row numbers for those rows. The same trick works for columns. Click on the column letter to select a single column or drag across the letters to select a group of columns.

Edit⇨Undo

Reverses your last action. Unfortunately, you can use this command to back up only a single step. If you press it a second time, it undoes the undo and you end up back where you started.

For mouse maniacs

Affectionately known as the "Help! Get me out of here!" button.

For keyboard krazies

[**Ctrl**] + [**Z**]

Just the facts

As long as you remember to do Undo immediately after a mistake, all you need to do is go to the menu and select the command. Or better yet, just use one of the shortcuts.

More stuff

The actual command name changes to indicate what the last action was (the one that can be undone). Typical command names are Undo Typing, Undo Cut, Undo Paste, and Undo Sort Go.

There are some actions that you cannot undo, such as saving a file. However, most anything you do by using the Block or Edit menu can be undone.

File⇨Close

Closes the current notebook. If you've made changes, you are asked if you want to save them.

For mouse maniacs

 Double-click in the document control box to close the current object. If the document window is maximized, the document control box is below the program control box. Otherwise, it's at the left of the title bar. The bar in the document control box is slightly smaller than the one for the program. Double-clicking the program control box exits Quattro Pro.

For keyboard krazies

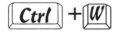

Just the facts

An amazingly easy-to-use command. The only thing that will probably happen is that you will be asked whether you want to save your changes when you try to close a notebook. If you want to keep the changes, click on <u>Y</u>es. If you want to throw them out (and go back to what you had when you last saved), select <u>N</u>o.

More stuff

 If you're done working with Quattro Pro, you can get ready to go home by using <u>F</u>ile⇨E<u>x</u>it. If you want to reference a notebook without having it clutter up your screen, you can use <u>W</u>indow⇨<u>H</u>ide.

File⇨Exit

Closes up everything (including the actual program) so that you can go home for the day. If you've made changes other than to the contents of any of the opened notebooks, you are asked whether you want to save the changes.

For mouse maniacs

Double-click the program control box, the one with the larger bar, to exit Quattro Pro. It's the one in the far upper-right corner of the program window.

For keyboard krazies

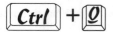

Just the facts

After you select File↪Exit, Quattro Pro starts closing down business. If you've made any changes that you haven't saved, you're given a chance to save them before Quattro Pro closes the window with the changes.

More stuff

For more on stopping and starting Quattro Pro, see Chapter 2 in *Quattro Pro 6 For Windows For Dummies.*

If you just want to get rid of the window for a single notebook, you can use File↪Close.

File ↪ List of Files

Lists your five most recently used notebooks so that you can open them quickly. Quattro Pro lists one more than most programs.

Just the facts

The fact that the most recently used notebooks are on the File menu is one of the most useful shortcuts in existence (particularly for authors who have to revise the same file over and over again). Alt, F, 1 opens the file used last — that is, the first one on the list.

More stuff

If you work with the same notebook all the time, it's position on the list should stay the same. However, if you work with a variety of notebooks (more than five), the names on the list and their positions may change as you work with the notebooks.

If your file is not on the list, you need to use File⇨Open.

Starts a new notebook to hold all your wonderful and insightful calculations. The new notebook is full of nothing but blank pages.

For mouse maniacs

 After one click of this button, a new notebook is there for you. Don't worry, your old notebook is just hidden behind the new one.

For keyboard krazies

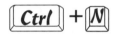

Just the facts

I don't think the programmers could make this command any easier to use. Just select it from the menu, click on the New Notebook button, or use the shortcut keys, and there you have it — a new, blank notebook.

More stuff

 If you have a notebook that contains most of the information and formatting that you need, you can "borrow" that information by making a copy of the notebook. To do this, first open the notebook that already has the information. Second, make a separate copy of the notebook under a new name by using the File⇨Save As command. Next, close the document and then reopen the one with the new name by using File⇨Open. In most cases, you can skip this last step, but I like to do it anyway to make sure that I have a complete copy that will open. Get rid of the information you don't need and start adding the new stuff.

Use File⇨Open to open an existing notebook.

Opens any notebook for you. In fact, it even opens worksheets created in other programs.

For mouse maniacs

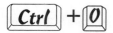

It's a good thing these buttons don't wear out because you'll use the Open button every time you change notebooks (unless the name of the notebook that you want to open already appears on the File menu).

For keyboard krazies

Ctrl + **O**

Just the facts

The only possible problem with this command is remembering where you stored the notebook. When you select File⇨Open, you're presented with a dialog box that lets you move around on your hard disk. After you locate the notebook file that you want, simply double-click on it to load it into Quattro Pro, and it opens to the first page.

When you are searching for a file, you can use the Drives list to change which disk you are looking at and the Directories list to move between directories on your disk. To move up a level, double-click on the opened folder. To move down a level, double-click on the closed folder. If you click once on a filename in the FileName list, the File Information area displays the date and time the file was last saved and the size of the file.

More stuff

If you are looking for files that were created by a program other than Quattro Pro, or if you have changed the extension for Quattro Pro's files by using Application⇨File Options, you may need to change which files are showing in the FileName list by selecting a different option from the List Files of Type list.

If the file you are trying to open is password protected (with the Active Notebook⇨Password Level command), you also have to provide the password to open the file. To open a protected file, use the normal steps for opening the file, but before the file is completely loaded, you are given a special dialog box where you need to type the proper password.

For more information about the File commands, see Chapter 7 in *Quattro Pro 6 For Windows For Dummies*. For more information about moving around on your disks, see *Windows For Dummies*.

Always check to see whether your file is listed at the bottom of the File menu. For more information on this shortcut, see File⮑*List of Files*. If you want to start with a blank notebook, use File⮑New. You may have a collection of notebooks saved together, in which case you need to use File⮑Workspace. To tell Quattro Pro where to first look for notebooks, use Application⮑File Options.

File ⮑ Page Setup

Tells Quattro Pro what type of paper you are using and how to format the notebook to fit. You can also use Page Setup to add headers and footers to each of your pages.

For mouse maniacs

The Margins button on the Print Preview SpeedBar takes you directly to the dialog box for setting margins.

The Setup button on the Print Preview SpeedBar takes you to the Page Setup dialog box, where you can change any of the setup settings.

Just the facts

This is another of those Quattro Pro commands with multiple personalities. On the left side of the dialog box is a series of five options plus two buttons. The buttons are used for storing your standard settings as the default. After you decide what settings you want for the various options, click on the Save Defaults button. Now, any time that you want to return to those settings, you can simply click on the Load Defaults button.

Although it's the last option, now is a good time to mention Named Settings. When you select this option, the rest of the dialog box changes to a list with a box labeled New Set and four buttons. You use this dialog box to store other collections of settings in addition to your default set. To create a new set, enter a name in the New Set text box and click on the Add button. To use an existing set, select it from the list and click on the Use button. If you want to make changes to a set, you generally load it with the Use button, go to the other options and make any changes you want, and then return to the Named Settings option and click on the Update button. To get rid of a set, select it from the list and click on the Delete button.

The other options control various parts of the page setup. The first option, Paper Type, controls what type of paper Quattro Pro assumes that you are using and whether the paper is to be used in Portrait orientation or Landscape orientation. In Portrait orientation, the page is read across the narrow edge — the same shape as a portrait in an art gallery. In Landscape orientation, the information goes along the longer edge — the same shape as a landscape painting. The types of paper available can vary depending upon which printer you have installed — a feature set by using the File⇨Print command.

The second option, Header/Footer lets you enter text to appear at the top of each page (Header) or at the bottom of each page (Footer). There are also two buttons for changing the fonts for each. These buttons reveal dialog boxes that bear a striking resemblance to the one you see with Active Block⇨Font.

The next option, Print Margins, lets you set the four page margins (Top, Bottom, Left, and Right) as well as the positions for the top of the Header and the bottom of the Footer. The Break Pages check box controls whether Quattro Pro pays any attention to the top and bottom margins. If the option is cleared, Quattro Pro does not print headers or footers and ignores any top or bottom margin. You end up with one long sheet of paper with printing all the way down it. This feature may be useful if you have a tractor-feed printer, but it doesn't help much with a laser printer (which has a 1/2-inch@bf margin on the edge where the print cannot print).

The last option, Print Scaling, has only two items. You can check Print to Fit to have Quattro Pro reduce the information to be printed so that it fits on a single page, or you can enter a scaling factor in the Scaling box.

More stuff

There are a variety of codes that you can use in your header or footer. The following table summarizes some of the most interesting codes.

Code	What It Does
I (vertical bar)	Separates each of the three portions of a header or footer: the far left, the center, and the far right. Any of the portions can be left blank. I I#d, for example, puts the date to the far right.

#n	Starts another line.
#d	Enters the current date in the short format specified in the Date Format option of Application⇨International. A capital *D* uses the long format. Add a lowercase *s* to use the standard short date (#ds) and long date (#Ds) formats.
#t	Enters the current time in the short format specified in the Time Format option of Application⇨International. The same options are available for the time format as are available for the date formats (#T, #ts, and #Ts).
#p	Enters the current page number.
#P	Enters the number of pages in the document.
#f	Enters the name of the notebook printing with no path (INFO.WB2). A capital *F* adds the path (C:\VERY\DEEPLY\BURIED\INFO.WB2).

The whole story about setting up your pages can be found in Chapter 11 in *Quattro Pro 6 For Windows For Dummies*.

Some of the other options which control how your printed page will look are found under File⇨Print. Perhaps the easiest way to format your printing options is to use File⇨Print Preview.

File⇨Print

Lets you control exactly what is printed, including which pages; what parts of the page are printed, such as the gridlines; and which rows and columns are used for headings. It also lets you decide which printer you are using and lets you change any printer options.

For mouse maniacs

On the Main SpeedBar, clicking on the Print button opens the Print dialog box. On the Print Preview SpeedBar, clicking on this button starts the printing itself.

On the Print Preview SpeedBar, clicking on the Options button opens the Sheet Options dialog box.

For keyboard krazies

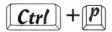

Just the facts

The most important items in the Print dialog box are those contained within the Print Area section. These options determine exactly what it is you are printing. Your choices are the Current Page, all the pages in the Notebook, or a Block Selection (which you could have highlighted before selecting the command or which you can change with the Point Mode button next to the text box).

The other section on the dialog box, Print Pages, interacts with the Print Area section. You can choose between printing All Pages within the print area or specifying a range with From and to values.

Use the Copies box to print as many copies as you need, but bear in mind that if you need more than a few, it's probably faster to use a copying machine.

Sounds pretty easy so far, but don't worry, the programmers hid the complexity. The Sheet Options button displays the rather complex Spreadsheet Print Options dialog box shown here.

Spreadsheet Print Options		
Headings	**Print Options**	OK
Top Heading:	☐ Cell Formulas	Cancel
	☐ Gridlines	
Left Heading:	☐ Row/Column Borders	Load Defaults
	☐ Center Blocks	Save Defaults
Print Between Blocks	**Print Between 3D Pages**	
◉ Lines 0	○ Lines: 0	Help
○ Page Advance	○ Page Advance	

The settings you are most likely to use are those in the Print Options section. Checking the first option, Cell Formulas, causes Quattro Pro to print the actual formulas rather than their results in each cell. The second, Gridlines, controls whether the gridlines between cells are printed. When checked, each cell is clearly outlined. This option has no effect on borders that you have created with Active Block⇨Line Drawing. Put a check next to the

Row/Column Borders option to print the letters and numbers for each column and row. You most often use this option when you want to print the formulas to try and track down a problem. The last of the Print Options, Center Blocks, formats the page so that the blocks of information are centered. This feature matters only if your block does not fill up the page.

The two text boxes at the upper left, Top Heading and Left Heading, allow you to select blocks of cells to be printed at the top and left of each page, respectively. This option is different from the header and footer settings in File⇨Page Setup. The headers and footers are the same for each page no matter what the contents of the page. The Top Heading is usually the first row or two of the spreadsheet, which is then repeated if there are rows that are forced onto a second page. The Left Heading is usually the first column and is repeated if there are columns that are placed onto a second page.

The Print Between Blocks sections and the Print Between 3D Pages sections let you control the spacing between parts of the notebook. You can have either a specified number of lines between each section or a page break. If you want a continuos look, enter 0 as the number of lines.

On the right side of the dialog box are two buttons used for storing your standard settings as the default. Click on the Save Defaults button after you've created settings for the various options that you want to save. Then you can click on the Load Defaults button any time you want to return to those settings.

The Print button actually starts your print job. The Close button is used only when you decide it was all a mistake, and you don't really want to print after all.

The first line at the top of the dialog box lists which printer you are currently using. You can change the printer by clicking on the Select Printer button and making the desired changes. Clicking on the Print Preview button is the same as having selected File⇨Print Preview. Clicking on Page Setup moves you to the same dialog box as appears for File⇨Page Setup.

More stuff

When you are printing a graph or slide show, the dialog box is organized differently. It's much smaller, and the Print Area and Print Pages sections are missing. You may also notice that there is no Sheet Options button. These features are unavailable when printing graphs and slides.

You can learn more about printing in Chapter 11 in *Quattro Pro 6 For Windows For Dummies*. The Select Printer button is actually a Windows feature discussed in *Windows For Dummies*.

Other options that control your output are found under File⇨Page Setup. You really should be ecological about printing and check your output by using File⇨Print Preview before printing. To have a heading row or column display on-screen, use View⇨Locked Titles.

File⇨Print Preview

Formats your notebook pages as they will be printed and provides the Print Preview SpeedBar. This command is probably the most ecological feature of the entire program.

For mouse maniacs

`Page 1 of 1`

By clicking in the Page Indicator box, you can type a page number into the box that appears and press Tab to jump to that page.

⬛ ⬛   You use these buttons to move forward or backward a single page.

⬛ ⬛   The Zoom buttons increase or decrease the magnification.

⬛   The Color button toggles between showing your page in color and in black and white.

⬛   Without the Exit Preview button, you'd be trapped in the Print Preview mode for the rest of your life.

Because what you see may not be what you want, there are buttons for moving to the Page Setup and Spreadsheet Print Options dialog boxes. The Margin and Setup buttons are discussed under File⇨Page Setup. The Options and Print buttons are discussed under File⇨Print.

Just the facts

Getting into Print Preview mode is easy. Go to the page you want to work in, highlight what it is you want to print, and then select File⇨Print Preview. It's what you do after you get in this mode that can be confusing.

Print Preview mode offers you a view of what your document will look like when it is printed. Use the Previous Page and Next Page buttons (or the Page Up and Page Down keys) to change which page you are looking at or to enter a page number in the Page Indicator box.

You can use the Zoom In button (or the plus key) to move closer to see the detail or the Zoom Out button (or the minus key) to move further away to get a better overall look. If the entire page isn't showing on-screen, you can use either the scroll bars or the arrow keys to move around on the page.

Because most people don't have a color printer, the Color button can be used to change the page into a black-and-white representation. It may be more boring, but it's also closer to what you'll see on your paper.

To get out of Print Preview mode, either click on the Exit Preview button or press Escape.

More stuff

For a review of Preview, see Chapter 11 in *Quattro Pro 6 For Windows For Dummies*.

In addition to the commands for formatting your spreadsheet, the look of your final printout is affected by settings under File⇨Page Setup and File⇨Print.

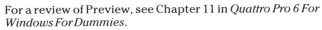

File ⇨ Publish

Magically converts your notebook into a best-selling novel. OK, it really doesn't, but that's a feature I'd pay big bucks for! Anyway, the File⇨Publish command actually makes the current notebook available to other users via the Object Exchange (OBEX). This is the sort of command you should not try to use unless someone in your office explains how it works on your network. In fact, this command won't be available on your system unless OBEX was installed.

Just the facts

You have to do many things before you can use this command — the sort of things that hopefully will be done by someone else. First, you must set up various accounts for your network with the OBEX program. In this case, an *account* means a method for exchanging information for a single person or group on the network. After you've set up and configured the OBEX stuff (*configure* means "make it work"), you have to create an address book using the Address Book Manager to give all the accounts normal looking names. If all that's been set up, you can publish pages from your notebook.

The first time you select File⇨Publish, you're presented with the Publish dialog box, where you enter a description of what it is you will be sharing, create a list of names of people who can look

at it, and decide which pages to share. In the dialog box, there is a
Names button, which lets you create the list of people that can
use the information in your address book (created with the
handy-dandy Address Book Manager just mentioned). You have a
choice between sharing All Named Pages and using the Select
button to pick which pages to share. Then use Version Depth to
decide how many editions of the published pages to keep around.
If this option is set to 1, only the current version is available. If the
option is set to 3, the current version plus the last two versions
that you published are available. You can keep up to 99 versions
available at one time.

After you've published something, use File⇨Publish to update the
versions manually and to make the following changes: which
pages are published, who gets the publication, and other management tasks. If you want to stop the publication of your pages,
click on the Clear button, which prevents any future subscription
and removes the current version. People who have already
subscribed to a copy, however, still have the information. You
have to get those copies back by hand.

More stuff

As soon as you use one of the OBEX commands (Publish or
Subscribe), a new page, labeled Workgroup, appears in your
notebook and contains a summary of all the OBEX activity for
that notebook. A single notebook may have multiple publications
and very often has multiple subscriptions.

Just like a publisher needs subscribers, to use File⇨Publish,
someone else needs to be using File⇨Subscribe. If you want to
just send somebody a copy of your current notebook as a mail
message, use File⇨Send.

File⇨Save

Stores a copy of the notebook under its current name. If the
notebook hasn't been saved before, this command is the same as
selecting File⇨Save As.

For mouse maniacs

Get in the habit of clicking on the Save button regularly to save
your work.

For keyboard krazies

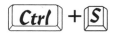

Just the facts

If you've already given your file a name, selecting File⇨Save updates the copy on disk. At that point, any changes become permanent. If you haven't already given the file a name, you're presented with the File⇨Save As dialog box, where you can decide where to store the file and what name to use.

More stuff

There's really no reason to use File⇨Save As unless you are changing the format of your file. If you haven't named your notebook, just select File⇨Save, and you get an opportunity.

To learn some good rules about saving your work, see Chapter 7 in *Quattro Pro 6 For Windows For Dummies*.

If you need to make changes to the filename or format, you should use File⇨Save As. If you have a group of notebooks you want to save together, use File⇨Workspace.

File⇨Save As

Gives you a chance to change the name or format of the file that contains your notebook. You can use File⇨Save As to make a copy of your notebook for other users less fortunate than yourself who don't have Quattro Pro 6.

Just the facts

To use the command, just select File⇨Save As. You get the Save As dialog box, with a number of options. The most important option is the name of the file, which goes in the FileName box. Don't worry about including an extension (the part after the period) because Quattro Pro provides that for you. Your filename can be up to eight characters long and can include any letter or number as well as some special characters (– and _ are very useful). You can't use spaces within the name. (That's what you use – and _ for!)

You can also select a file format from the Save File as Type list. When you save a file in another format, it is possible that some formatting or property information will be lost if the other program does not support the same features as Quattro Pro. If you intend to use a file with Quattro Pro, you should use the standard QPW v6 format when saving.

If you enter something in the Password Protection box, it is the same as setting the Active Notebook➪Password Level to High. Anyone wanting to open the notebook needs to provide the password.

More stuff

If a file already exists in the current direction with the same name you want to use for this new file, Quattro Pro provides a warning and asks whether it should Replace the file or Cancel the Save As action. In certain situations, it also gives you the option to Backup the file on disk by changing its extension to BAK.

For more information about the File commands (including using them to make backup copies), see Chapter 7 in *Quattro Pro 6 For Windows For Dummies*.

If you simply want to store your notebook on disk, use File➪Save. To save a group of notebooks together, use File➪Workspace.

File➪Send

Sends a copy of the current notebook to another user on your network as a mail message by using either your usual mail system or the Object Exchange (OBEX). You should probably use this command only if you have been cleared in its use by your network guru. In fact, the command may not even appear on your File menu depending upon whether you installed OBEX or a mail program.

Just the facts

What you see after selecting File➪Send depends upon the type of network mail system you have available. If you are already using a mail system on your network, File➪Send provides access to that system and adds the capability to mail notebook pages as attachments to your messages. In most cases, the recipient can use either your normal mail system or the File➪Subscribe command to recover the notebook pages.

If you don't have a mail system but you do have a network, File⇨Send uses OBEX to send your messages. As briefly summarized under File⇨Publish, someone (hopefully, not you) needs to have set up OBEX accounts and address books. With OBEX, you get the Object Exchange: Send dialog box, where you can insert an Address from your OBEX Address Book in the To and the Cc boxes. You can also enter a description on the Subject line and your own text in the Message box. The current notebook is automatically included as an attachment. You can use the Add button to include other attachments and the Remove button to get rid of any selected attachment.

More stuff

Rather than just sending off a copy, you can give someone ongoing access to your work by publishing it with File⇨Publish.

File⇨Subscribe

Connects you to a notebook that has been either sent directly to you or published by someone else using the Object Exchange (OBEX). This command is one of those super-secret network commands that you should check out with your local guru and won't be available unless OBEX is installed.

Just the facts

In order to do anything with OBEX, someone has to have gone through all the work of setting up the OBEX accounts and address books (see File⇨Publish for a very brief overview). The first thing you should do if you're going to subscribe is to make sure that your listing of publications is current. To update your list, select Tools⇨Object Exchange⇨Poll Now. You should also be in the notebook where you want to insert the pages.

When you select File⇨Subscribe, you are presented with the Use Notebooks and Pages dialog box. If you want the dialog box to include your own publications, put a check next to Show Publications. As you click on each item in the Description list, the Contents, Distributed By, and Last Distributed information is put in the bottom of the dialog box. Find the item that you want in the list and select it.

Several choices are available for what information you actually insert and how you insert it. The first choice is whether you want the Current version or whether you want to go Back several versions. The second choice is whether you want Automatic updates of new versions or whether you want to be responsible for doing Manual updates. Finally, you can use the Select Pages button to include only a portion of the publication. After you've set these features, select Insert, and the pages are placed into your notebook.

To get rid of a publication from the list, select it and click on the Delete button.

More stuff

If your notebook already contains a page with the same name as a page in the publication, Quattro Pro changes the publication page's name to keep it unique. For lettered pages, it puts an underscore in front of the letter (so F becomes _F). Quattro Pro adds a number after named pages.

When you use File⇨Subscribe to add pages to your notebook, the Workgroup page is added to your notebook. This special page is maintained by Quattro Pro and contains a summary of all the OBEX activity for that notebook by listing any publications and all subscriptions.

To have a subscription, someone else must have used File⇨Publish.

File⇨Workspace

Saves or retrieves a set of notebooks as a single workspace. This command is particularly useful for more advanced users who may want to load several notebooks that include macro libraries and system notebooks. Most of us normal folk don't need to worry about this command.

Just the facts

There are two commands, called *submenus*, located off to the side of Workspace. The Save command lets you store a collection of notebooks as a workspace. The Restore command loads all the files within the collection in a single step by selecting the workspace you want to use from the dialog box.

The File⇨Workplace⇨Save command works just like File⇨Save As and includes any and all open notebooks in the workspace.

More stuff

A workspace file has the extension WBS.

For an explanation of how you can use this command, see Chapter 7 in *Quattro Pro 6 For Windows For Dummies*.

If you just need to save a single notebook, use File⇨Save. To open a notebook, use File⇨Open.

Graphics⇨Delete Graph

Removes a graph from existence. This command is also called the "Terminator 2000" command. If you just want to remove the copy of the graph from the notebook page, select it and then press Delete.

Just the facts

Be careful! This command actually removes the graph from the Objects Page. After you select Graphics⇨Delete Graph, you get the Delete Graph dialog box, which lists all the graphs in the current notebook. Highlight the graph you want to blow away (get rid of) and click on OK. You don't get any more warning — that graph is history.

More stuff

To remove a copy of the graph from a notebook page, select the graph and then use Edit⇨Clear.

Graphics⇨Edit Graph

Opens a graph for editing. This command lets you make changes to the various objects that make up the graph, such as the x-axis, the colors, and the background.

Just the facts

Selecting the Graphics⇨Edit Graph command displays a dialog box where you can select the graph you want to edit. It doesn't matter whether the graph has been inserted onto a notebook page because the graph is opened into its own window.

After a graph is opened for editing, you can select the various aspects of the graph to make changes. The things you can select include such things as Graph Setup and Background Properties for all types of graphs; Pie Graph Properties for a pie chart; and Bar Series Properties, Area Fill Properties, and Legend Properties for a bar graph. To get to the properties for a component, put the cursor over the item (such as one of the slices in a pie chart), click the right mouse button, and select the first item from the pop-up menu.

Each of the Properties dialog boxes contains a variety of choices. For example, the Graph Setup and Background Properties dialog box contains options for setting the style of box around the graph, the color of the box, the color and fill pattern for the background, as well as choices for changing the graph type. Selecting an item that represents data (such as a slice in a pie chart or a bar in a bar chart) lets you change the color and pattern used, the border of the item, and a wide variety of settings associated with the label.

The only way to really learn to use all the features is to experiment. If your only concern is in creating a graph that is both attractive and reasonably representative of your data, you should use the Advisor discussed as part of the Edit⇨Graph Gallery command.

More stuff

The Font and Font Size lists on the Property Band may also be used to change the font properties of titles. The third list, normally Styles, changes to Color Sets. You can select a color scheme from this list to change the colors for all the items in the graph. You can also use the Palette toolbar to change the color of any selected item.

You can also select Edit or Open from the menu that appears when you click once with the right mouse button within an inserted graph on a notebook page.

You can edit a graph that has been inserted onto a notebook page by double-clicking on the graph. To return to working with the notebook, click once outside the graph region. You can also change the border around the inserted graph by using options available on the Graph dialog box. To get to the Graph dialog box, click on the inserted graph once with the right mouse button and then select Graph Properties from the pop-up menu, or you can select the graph and then select Current Object from the Properties list.

You can set two sets of properties for a graph window by right-clicking on the title bar of the window (or by selecting GraphWindow from the Properties list). This opens the Graph Window dialog box. If you click on Aspect Ratio in the list on the left of the dialob box, the choices duplicate the commands on the View menu. If you click on Grid in the list to the left, the dialog box lets you activate an invisible grid for aligning objects. Actually, if you put a check next to Display Grid, the grid is visible, but it isn't when you start. To turn on the grid for aligning objects, put a check next to Snap to Grid. You can change the spacing of the grid by using the Grid Size slider.

To add a new graph, use Graphics⇨New Graph. To place a graph on the notebook page, use Graphics⇨Insert Graph. You can use Edit⇨Paste Special to copy some of the properties of one graph to another.

Graphics⇨Edit Slide Show

Takes you to the filmstrip view, which allows you to reorganize the graphs used within a slide show and control the special effects used to move from one slide to another.

For mouse maniacs

Clicking the Edit Slide Show button lets you select the slide show to edit and displays the Slide Show menu and the Slides SpeedBar.

Just the facts

When you select Graphics⇨Edit Slide Show, you get a little dialog box that lets you pick from a list of all your existing slide shows. You can either double-click on a slide show name or select one of the names and select OK to open the slide show for editing. You can select any of the slides and change the transition effects by using the same techniques that are discussed under Slide Show⇨Insert Slide. Slide shows are presented for editing in what I call the *filmstrip view*. To see an example, look at the figure in Graphics⇨New Slide Show.

More stuff

For the mechanics of creating the transitions for your slide show, see Slide Show⇨Edit Slide. To see the results of your editing, use Graphics⇨Run Slide Show or Slide Show⇨Run Slide Show. To edit a single slide, use Slide Show⇨Edit Slide or, if you are working with the graph, Graphics⇨Edit Graph.

Provides a vast, almost infinite, selection of choices for formatting your graph. Perhaps even more important is that this command provides an Advisor to help you select a format that makes sense.

For mouse maniacs

The Graph Gallery button takes you to the Graph Gallery, where you can pick a format for your graph.

Just the facts

The Graph Gallery is one of the neatest features in all of Quattro Pro. When you first select the command, you get the Graph Gallery dialog box. In the upper-left corner is the Category list. Your choices are Bar, Rotated Bar, Pie, Line or Area, Specialty, and Templates. The last choice, Templates, is used with bulleted lists. When you select any of the other choices, the Style area displays examples of the various types of graphs within that category. As you move through the various examples, you can click on them to see a preview of your graph in the area to the right. Notice that the Style area has a scroll bar that you can use to view additional choices.

You can use the list under Color Scheme to select a color palette for your graph. The only way to learn the effects you can create with the different color schemes is by experimenting.

The really neat-o feature is the Advisor button near the lower-right corner of the dialog box. After you click on this button, you get the Graph Advisor shown in the figure.

Graph Advisor	
Constraints	**Suggestions**
Individual ◄ ——— ► Cumulative	
Differences ◄ ——— ► Trends	
Simple ◄ ——— ► Fancy	
Data Columns: 3 ▲▼ Data Rows: 3 ▲▼	
Apply Cancel	Advise Help

The first of the three slider bars is used to represent how much you want the graph to show each Individual value within the group. In general, a line chart emphasizes individual values, and a stacked bar emphasizes the cumulative value for the group.

The second slider controls the emphasis on showing the Differences within the groups versus showing Trends for the group. Combo charts are often used to separate the groups so that the differences within each are emphasized. On the other hand, line and area charts are used for showing trends.

The third slider moves between Simple and Fancy. Keep in mind that a fancy graph often makes it difficult to see your point.

There are also boxes for indicating how many Data Columns and Data Rows are to be represented by the graph.

After you've decided on a setting for each of these options, click on the Advise button to see four suggested graph formats. If you like one of the formats, select it and then click on the Apply button. Otherwise, go back and make changes to the settings for some or all the options and try again.

More stuff

You can change the color scheme for an existing graph by selecting any part of the graph and then using the third list on the Property Band (the Palette list).

For a tour of some pretty fancy graphs, see Chapter 13 in *Quattro Pro 6 For Windows For Dummies.*

The biggest disadvantage to the Graph Gallery is that you must have an existing graph that you created by using the Graphics⇨New Graph command. To change the type of graph without using the Graph Gallery, use Graphics⇨Type. To add titles to your graph, use Graphics⇨Titles. You can change the look of elements within the graph by using Graphics⇨Edit Graph.

Graphics⇨Insert Graph

Adds an existing graph onto the notebook page. You get a dialog box asking you to pick a graph and then a cursor which lets you draw a box for positioning the graph you selected.

Just the facts

First, go to the notebook page where you want to place one of
your existing graphs. After you select Graphics⇨Insert Graph,
you get a list of all the available graphs. You can either double-
click on the graph name or select the name and then select OK.
As soon as you choose the graph, the dialog box closes, and you
are left with a cursor that resembles a big plus sign with a graph
to the lower left. Use this cursor to draw a rectangular boundary
at the place where you want the graph inserted. To draw the
boundary, go to where you want one of the corners, hold down
the mouse button, and drag to where you want the opposite
corner. In mere moments, the rectangle is filled with the selected
graph.

More stuff

To create a graph and insert it in a single step, use the Graph Tool
button described under Graphics⇨New Graph.

Graphics⇨New Graph

Creates a new graph object. If you have a block of cells selected,
Quattro Pro tries to use the selected information to create the
graph. If you don't have anything selected, you are presented
with a very intimidating dialog box.

For mouse maniacs

If you use the Graph Tool button, you can create and position the
graph in a single step.

Just the facts

Rarely have I seen such a difference between using a menu
command and using its related button. Although they both create
a new graph, where they put the graph is very different. Use the
button to put a graph onto a notebook page. Use the command to
create a graph in its own window. Both techniques create a graph
object on the Objects Page. To help keep the difference straight,
the button's pop-up name is Graph Tool.

To start with either technique, highlight the block of information
that you want to use to create your graph. If your block has labels
for identifying the rows and columns, be sure to include them.

If you click on the New Graph button, you get a cursor with a plus sign and a little picture of a graph. You can use this cursor to drag a rectangle on the page where you want to insert the graph. If you use the command, you get a rather frightening dialog box. Don't worry. It won't hurt. Just select OK. You should now have an attractive and (hopefully) useful graph.

More stuff

If your notebook page is organized so that the information that you want to use to create your graph isn't side by side, you can highlight separate blocks of cells to create your graph. First, highlight the column of labels. If you intend to include the label for the column of values, be sure to highlight the corresponding cell in the first column. Then, hold down the Ctrl key and highlight the column of data. You should make sure that each separate block you highlight is the same size and shape. This trick doesn't always work, but it's worth trying. Your other choices are to rearrange your table or to use Graph⇨Series to define the graph by hand.

You can also use the SpeedMenu by first selecting the cell(s) and then clicking the right mouse button (while the cursor is over the selection). You see a nifty pop-up menu where you can select the New Graph command. This technique creates a new graph on the Objects Page.

To find out more about changing the way the graph uses your data, see Chapter 13 in *Quattro Pro 6 For Windows For Dummies*.

To add an existing graph to a notebook page, use Graphics⇨Insert Graph.

Graphics⇨New Slide Show

Lets you create a new slide show and then add slides to it. To work with a slide show, you need to use the Slide Show menu and the Slides SpeedBar.

For mouse maniacs

The New Slide Show button is available on the toolbar for the Objects Page or the toolbar you get when you are editing a slide show.

Just the facts

Right after you select the Graphics⟶New Slide Show command
(or, for that matter, the Slide Show⟶New Slide Show command),
you are presented with a dialog box where you are asked to name
the slide show. Provide a name that describes what the series of
slides is about and then select OK. You are now looking at what I
call the *filmstrip view*. Doesn't it look like an old-fashioned
filmstrip to you?

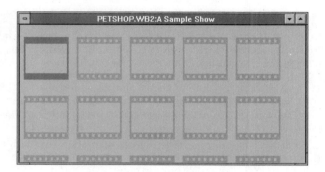

You can use each of the blank rectangles to hold one of your
slides. You now need to position your slides (which are graphs
dressed up for presentation) and decide on the transitions
between each pair. The steps for doing this are described under
Slide Show⟶Insert Slide because that's the command you have to
use to build your slide show.

More stuff

A slide show is a series of slides that you can present either on-
screen or by printing to use with other technology (including
printing back-and-white images on paper). For the most part, it's
easier to create all the graphs that you want to use in your slide
show first. Make sure to give each graph a name that lets you
recognize the contents later. Then go to a blank page in your
notebook and enter any information that you want to present as
lists within your slide show. Finally, use Slide Show⟶Insert Slide
and Slide Show⟶New Slide to build your actual slide show.

The mechanics of how a slide show is put together is discussed
under Slide Show⟶Insert Slide. To change an existing slide show,
use Graphics⟶Edit Slide Show. To add a slide to a slide show, use
either Slide Show⟶Insert Slide or Slide Show⟶New Slide. You
control how the slide show is displayed by using the commands
on the View menu.

Graphics⇨Run Slide Show

Makes that slide show a reality by moving you from one slide to another — complete with your desired special effects and timing. It's way too cool.

For mouse maniacs

The Run Slide Show button is available on the toolbar for the Objects Page or the toolbar you get when you are editing a slide show.

Just the facts

When you select Graphics⇨Run Slide Show, you're presented with a dialog box that lists all the existing slide shows. Double-click on one or select its name and then select OK to start the presentation. If the delay for the slides is set at 0.0, you have to click once on the screen to move from slide to slide. If the delay has been set to a value, after the specified number of seconds, Quattro Pro automatically moves to the next slide. Even if the delay has been set, you can still go ahead and click to immediately move on.

More stuff

Create a slide show with Graphics⇨New Slide Show. The mechanics of how a slide show is put together is discussed under Slide Show⇨Insert Slide.

Graphics⇨Series

Changes the information used to create the selected graph. Of course, you need to be careful, or you can distort your graph so much that it is unrecognizable.

Just the facts

The information used to create a graph actually consists of a bunch of block addresses organized in a special format. To see the Graph Series dialog box, which controls what goes where, select Graphics⇨Series.

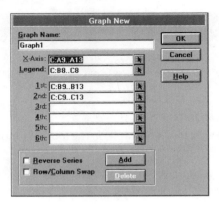

The two boxes at the top of the dialog box, X-Axis and Legend, usually refer to blocks that contain labels. Almost all types of graphs have an *x-axis*. In a pie or doughnut chart, the x-axis includes the labels for the slices. In a bar chart, the x-axis includes the labels for the groups of bars (the first group may have a red, blue, and green bar). In other charts, the x-axis is the axis along the bottom. Except for pie charts and doughnut charts, most charts also have a legend. The *legend* is the name that describes each line, or the objects in the graph of the same color (all the blue bars, for example).

The boxes labeled 1st, 2nd, and so on are where you put the blocks that contain the actual data or values for the graph. If you need to describe more groups, you can click on the Add button to get additional boxes. If there are more boxes than you need, you can either leave them blank, or you can click in the one you want to get rid of and then click on the Delete button.

Put a check next to the Reverse Series option to reverse the order of the groups in the legend. Choosing this option causes the series at the front of the graph to move to the back. This option is particularly useful when you are working with a 3-D graph, and the groups in the front are covering up those in the back. To change the order within the legend, you have to rearrange the information on your notebook page.

Putting a check next to Row/Column Swap causes the x-axis and the legend to be switched. If your graph showed the changes in three products over the past three years (with each product being represented by a color), checking Row/Column Swap changes your graph so that it shows the change over the last three years for each of the products (with each year being represented by a color).

More stuff

After you're in the Graph Series dialog box, you can use the little button (called the Point Mode button) to the right of the text boxes to select the block on your spreadsheet. After you click on the button, the dialog box is reduced to just a title bar. Select the cells you want from the spreadsheet and then double-click on the dialog box title bar. See the "Just the facts" section of the Block⟹Copy command for a visual example of the Point Mode button. If your notebook is showing, you also can simply click anywhere on the page, highlight a block, and be immediately returned to the dialog box.

You can also select Series from the menu that appears when you click once within the graph region with the right mouse button.

To find out more about changing the way the graph uses your data, see Chapter 13 in *Quattro Pro 6 For Windows For Dummies*.

It's often easier to start over by using Graphics⟹New Graph than it is to change the series. If you want to add or change the titles on your graph, use Graphics⟹Titles.

Graphics⟹*Titles*

Gives you a chance to title your masterpiece with both a main title and a subtitle. You can also add titles for the x-axis and the y-axis. If you're using a combination graph, you can even add a second y-axis title.

Just the facts

Selecting Graphics⟹Titles displays a dialog box where you can enter the text to be used for Main Title (which appears centered at the top of the graph) and the Subtitle (which appears below the main title). Depending upon the type of graph you are using, you may also be able to add text for the X-Axis Title, the Y1-Axis Title (on the left) and the Y2-Axis Title (on the right of combination charts). After you've entered your text, just select OK to add it to the graph. You can select the command at any time to make changes to the text.

More stuff

To format the titles, move the cursor over the text and click once with the right mouse button. Next, select the first item on the pop-up menu, something like GraphTitleBox Properties. The resulting dialog box has a wide variety of formatting options. Have fun and experiment.

After you've added titles, you can edit the graph by using the Graphics⇨Edit Graph command and then move the titles by using the mouse. Simply click on the title you want to move and drag it to the new location. The main title and subtitle must be moved together.

 The items on the Property Band may also be used to change the font properties of titles.

 You can also select Titles from the menu that appears when you click once within the graph region with the right mouse button.

 Changing the type of graph with either the Graphics⇨Graph Gallery or the Graphics⇨Type command changes what titles are available on the graph.

Graphics⇨Type

Changes the type of graph you are using. While not as impressive as the Graph Gallery, the Graph Types dialog box actually offers more choices. Be sure to check out some of the cool combination graphs that are available.

Just the facts

The Graph Types dialog box has buttons that represent all 50 of the Quattro Pro graph types. The buttons are organized into six groups. To find out what any graph is called, simply click on the graph button and the name for that type of graph appears at the bottom of the dialog box.

The last group, Blank, creates the most boring type of graph possible. The graph doesn't have a thing on it. You primarily use this kind of graph for notes within a slide show or for creating a master slide.

The next to the last group, Bullet, takes a block containing text and converts it into a bulleted list for use in a slide show. The first column should contain your title and any subtitle. The next column contains the major points for the list, and the third column contains the subpoints, if any.

The first two categories, 2-D and 3-D, actually have the same basic graph types, but they look different when they're three-dimensional. The graph types range from pie charts to doughnut charts to spider webs, from line charts to bar charts, and from stacked bars to area charts. There is an additional 3-D graph — a 3-D floating marker graph.

The graphs in the Rotate group are like the bar charts and stacked bars in the 2-D and 3-D groups, except that the bars run across the page instead of up and down.

The final group to be discussed is the Combo group. The first three graphs in this group combine two graph types on a single graph. You usually use this type of combination graph when you are talking about two related trends that are on different scales or when you want to emphasize one of your groups. The remaining graphs are intended to compare the breakdown of separate groups. For example, there is an option for putting several pie charts (one for each group) onto the same graph.

More stuff

You can also select Type from the menu that appears when you click once within the graph region with the right mouse button.

You can get help deciding what type of graph to use and change the entire look of the graph by using Graphics⇨Graph Gallery. To change elements within the graph, use Graphics⇨Edit Graph.

Causes your graph to expand until it takes up the entire screen. With the expanded graph, you can see what the graph actually looks like without the usual screen clutter, such as menus and scroll bars.

For keyboard krazies

[F11]

Just the facts

Boy, is this an easy command. If you are working with a graph, just select Graphics⇨View Graph, and everything but your graph disappears, and your graph gets much bigger. In fact, it takes up the whole screen.

"How do I make it smaller again?" you might ask. Well, because you've been such a nice reader, I'll tell you. Either click the mouse button or press Escape.

If you aren't currently working with a graph when you select the command, you get a dialog box where you can pick which graph to view.

More stuff

You can also select View from the menu that appears when you click once with the right mouse button within an inserted graph on a notebook page.

Other commands that change the way the graph is displayed include <u>V</u>iew⇨<u>3</u>5mm Slide, <u>V</u>iew⇨<u>F</u>loating Graph, <u>V</u>iew⇨<u>P</u>rinter Preview, and <u>V</u>iew⇨<u>S</u>creen Slide.

<u>H</u>elp⇨<u>A</u>bout Quattro Pro

Tells you the version of Quattro Pro you are using and the date that it was created. This information comes in very handy when you have to deal with technical support.

Just the facts

All you can really do with this command is select <u>H</u>elp⇨<u>A</u>bout Quattro Pro, look at the information, and then select OK. That's it. It's not one of the more interesting commands.

More stuff

To learn more about the program, use one of the other Help commands, such as <u>H</u>elp⇨<u>C</u>oaches or <u>H</u>elp⇨<u>E</u>xperts.

<u>H</u>elp⇨<u>C</u>oaches

Provides advice and examples as you learn how to use Quattro Pro. This command is the new and improved coach who doesn't yell at you if you drop the ball.

For mouse maniacs

Doesn't that cap make the Coach look silly?

Just the facts

You can use the <u>H</u>elp⇨<u>C</u>oaches command in two ways: to learn new skills or to work through a problem with a notebook. If you are working through a problem, you need to start with the notebook that's giving you headaches. Select the <u>C</u>oaches command from the <u>H</u>elp menu to start getting relief.

The opening screen for the Coaches command displays five major headings on the left side: Essentials, Entering & Editing Data, Modifying Notebooks, Printing, and Graphics. As you select a major heading on the left, the list of topics on the left changes. When you find a topic that looks interesting (or which may help with your current crisis), click on the button next to the topic name to start that Coach.

The first Coaches screen describes what you'll learn and how to move through the Coach. Click on the red X to move back to the opening screen. The second Coaches screen usually asks whether you want to work with the Coach in your current notebook or in a sample notebook. If you're using the Coach to try and work through a problem, you'll want to use the current notebook containing the problem. If you're learning new skills or just practicing, go ahead and use the sample notebook.

Each of the remaining screens tells you how to perform a task and gives you the opportunity to try it within the notebook. You can continue practicing each task until you feel comfortable. The Coach guides you through the proper series of steps (in the proper order) to reach your goal.

If you want to quit working with the Coach, click on the button with the red X until you are returned to the opening screen and then click on the Quit button.

More stuff

The major problem with Coaches is that they require a lot of memory and system resources. In other words, they may run very slowly or not at all on most systems. The minor problem is that they require a mouse to get the most from the lessons.

Of course, it's nice if someone else will do the work for you. To get Quattro Pro to do your formatting, take a look at SpeedFormat. For more complex tasks, you might try looking at the Help➪Experts command.

Help➪Contents

Takes you to the table of contents for the Quattro Pro help file. From there, you can follow topics throughout the hypertext system.

For keyboard krazies

If you are just staring at the screen, F1 takes you directly to the Contents page for the Help file. If you are in the middle of a task, this shortcut takes you to the most appropriate entry (in the Help file designer's opinion).

Just the facts

When you're at the Help Contents page, you have a couple of choices. The most common approach is to browse your way through the Help system by clicking on one of the underlined, green topics. In general, the topics get more complex as you go down the list, but don't overlook the last one. Using Help gives you a quick introduction to using the Help system.

Going back to the start with Essentials provides information about the key features of the program as well as information about the new features in version 6. The next choice, How Do I, takes you to a series of topics that are oriented around how to do tasks. The next to the last topic, Additional Help, provides detailed information about each menu command, dialog box, and object within Quattro Pro. For each of these topics, the first few pages is a more focused table of contents for that topic and contains more underlined green topics that you can use to move closer to your information. Eventually, you get to page that actually tells you how to do what you want.

The @Functions topic takes you to a table of contents page where you can choose between going to a Function Index or finding the function you need by working through a list of categories. There are also a series of step-by-step instructions on Using @Functions and a topic for getting detailed information on @Function Arguments. An *argument* is the stuff that goes within the parentheses. For example, Q15..Z12 is the argument of the following @Function: @Sum(Q15..Z12).

The Macro topic takes you to a similar table of contents page for the commands that you can use within macros. This is Quattro Pro's programming language reference.

Each Help screen contains more underlined green topics, which you can use to move through the information. In addition, many pages include a "see also" list at the bottom that consists of related topics. You'll also find various terms marked with a dotted underline. These words are in the Glossary, and clicking on them reveals a short definition.

More stuff

Most of the time, you can get to the topic you need faster by starting the task and then pressing F1. F1 activates context-sensitive Help, which means that the Help system tries to guess what you're having problems with and moves to a related Help entry. In addition, many dialog boxes also have a Help button that you can push for information about that dialog box.

For more information on getting the help you need, see Chapter 2 in *Quattro Pro 6 For Windows For Dummies*.

It's easier to find something if you know what it is, so you may want to use the features described under Help ⇨ *Identify Command*.

Help ⇨ Experts

Actually performs the tasks for you after you answer a series of questions. If these "experts" were another series of programs by a company based in Redmond, WA (near the author), they would be called Wizards (and would look and act a bit differently).

For mouse maniacs

Click on the light bulb for inspiration from the experts.

Just the facts

When you select the Help ⇨ Experts command from the menu, it displays a submenu with eight choices: Analysis Tools, Budget, Consolidate, Graph, Performance, Scenario, Slide Show, and What-If. If you use the Experts buttons, you see a dialog box with the same choices. The dialog box is much prettier, but using the menus is faster. Each of the Experts covers a different topic, but they all work in basically the same way. Each screen asks you to respond to one or more questions and usually gives you a list of options to choose from. After you have worked your way through all the screens, the Expert goes out and performs the task as instructed by you.

The Graph and Slide Show Experts help you create objects in the current notebook. With the Graph Expert, if you select a block of data before starting the Expert, that block is used as the basis for the graph. Otherwise, you are guided through the steps of selecting the block and formatting the graph. Personally, I prefer using this Expert without selecting a block first. The Slide Show Expert is useful only if you want a slide show containing bulleted lists. Of course, you can use this Expert to create a slide show with lists and then change the lists into other types of graphs.

Several of the Experts are designed to simplify the commands that also appear on the menus. The Analysis Expert guides you through the use of the 19 tools for financial, statistical, and engineering analysis that are contained on the Tools⇨Numeric Tools⇨Analysis Tools dialog box. The Consolidate Expert helps you use the Tools⇨Consolidate command. You need to enter the values and formulas (or the data conditions and the results) before starting this Expert. The What-If Expert covers the use of the Tools⇨Numeric Tools⇨What-If feature. The Scenario Expert helps you use the Scenario Manager on the Tools menu.

The Performance Expert helps determine if the Compiled Formulas option (under Active Notebook⇨Recalc Settings) will speed up calculation times with your particular hardware and notebooks.

Finally, the Budget Expert gives you five different budget templates for home or business use.

More stuff

While you're learning Quattro Pro or when you run into a problem with a notebook, you may want to take advantage of Help⇨Coaches. For creating formulas, you can use Tools⇨Formula Composer; and for formatting, you can use SpeedFormat.

Help⇨Identify Button or List

Takes you directly to the Help topic associated with a particular command. This feature is a more useful approach if you are just trying to figure out what something is used for.

For mouse maniacs

Although Balloon Hints aren't actually part of the Help system, they are very useful for identifying the purpose of a button. If Balloon Hints are active (which they are unless you turn them off), holding the cursor over a button causes the button name to appear.

Just the facts

To get the Balloon Hint to appear for a button or a list, just hold the cursor over the item until the hint appears. If it seems like you are waiting forever, try clicking on the notebook and then going back over the button or list.

To get a bit more information than what is provided by the hint, you can hold down the Ctrl key and click on the item. You get a Help message like the one in the figure.

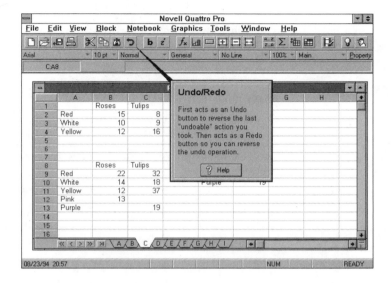

If you need further help, keep holding down the right mouse button and move the cursor until it's over the Help button. Then click with the left mouse button. Fortunately, you don't have to keep holding down the Ctrl key while you do all of this.

More stuff

To turn off the Balloon Hints, use Application⇨Display or View⇨Display.

Before resorting to the Help system for a menu item, try looking at the Help message in the title bar. These short messages are often enough to get you started in figuring out what a command actually does. The message displays while the menu item is highlighted.

See Help⇨Contents for a discussion of the context-sensitive Help system.

Help⇨Search

Goes through the Help file looking for topics that match the words that you provide. The only problem is that you have to guess what key words the author used within the Help system to identify particular topics. Fortunately, the list in the Search dialog box contains all these terms.

Just the facts

After you've open the Search dialog box (either by selecting Help⇨Search or by clicking the Search button from within Help), you are presented with an unlabeled text box in the upper-left corner, where you enter what you're looking for.

Start typing either a word or a phrase that describes what you are looking for. As you type, the Help system displays the closest matching phrase. If none of the suggested phrases is quite what you need, try deleting what you've typed and using a different phrase.

When you find a phrase that seems to describe what you want, click on the Show Topics button, which lists all the Help entries that are associated with that phrase. Look through the list for the phrase that seems closest to the one you want and click on it. The topics listed are generally related, and you can move between them. You can also select the Search button from any topic, and it returns you to the list you started from.

More stuff

You can get a lot of information by using the techniques described under Help⇨*Identify Button or List.*

Notebook⇨Combine

Used to take information from one notebook to another. You have the choice of inserting the new information, replacing the original information, or combining the information.

Just the facts

Before using Notebook⇨Combine, move to the cell that is at the upper-left corner of where you want to insert the new cells. Then go ahead and select the command. Although the File Combine dialog box looks a bit complex, it's actually fairly simple to use.

The most important section in the dialog box is the one labeled Operation, which you use to decide what to do with the cells that you are bringing into the notebook. The choices are pretty self-explanatory. Copy from New to Current just inserts the new cells starting at the current cursor location. If there aren't enough blank cells for the block you're inserting, Quattro Pro just writes the new information on top of the old — which ends up getting rid of the old information.

The other four operations combine the values in the new block and the values in the old. Quattro Pro looks only at the positions of the cells, so any labels are ignored. Because of this situation, make sure that your starting corner is in the right place before selecting the command. Your four choices are as follows:

- Add New to Current (which means New + Current)
- Subtract New from Current (which means Current – New)
- Multiply Current by New (which means New * Current)
- Divide Current by New (which means Current / New)

The entire left side of the dialog box is devoted to selecting the file. This section works just like the section in the dialog box for File⇨Open. After you select the file, you can use the Source section in the lower-right corner to decide between bringing in the cells from the Entire File or only those cells you list in the Block(s) box. When listing the cells you want to combine, you can use block addresses or named blocks. Be sure to check that you have the right option selected for the operation before starting the combination by selecting OK or double-clicking on the filename.

More stuff

For more complex combinations within a notebook, you should use Tools⇨Consolidator. Other methods for bringing information into a notebook include Notebook⇨Insert and Notebook⇨Text Import.

Notebook ⇨ Define Group

Creates a group of pages that share formatting and other property information. Think of it as a neighborhood with blocks of tract housing. Each page in the group is linked to all the other pages in the group. Even when pages are assigned to a group, however, you can still make individual changes.

Just the facts

After you understand the purpose of groups, defining and using them is really quite easy. The pages that are bound together in a group can be formatted individually or so that the formatting applies to each page in the group. Now you can be sure that each page of your notebook has a consistent look without giving up the flexibility of formatting individual pages.

To use groups, you first need to create them by using Notebook⇨Define Group. After you select the command, you see a dialog box with three boxes for entering information and a list of any existing groups. First, come up with a name for your group and put it in the Group Name box. Then, enter the name (or letter) for the First Page in its box and the Last Page in its box. After you select OK, the group is defined. To use the group, select View⇨Group Mode.

You can change the pages within the group by opening the dialog box and entering new values for the First Page or Last Page option or both. You can get rid of a group definition by selecting it from the list and clicking on the Delete button.

More stuff

The only restrictions are that the pages must all fall together within the notebook, and two groups can't overlap. For example, you can't put pages F and L in a group without including all the pages in between. Nor can you have one group for pages A through D and another group for pages D through G. Both groups can't include the same page — D, in this case.

To use the groups you've defined, choose View⇨Group Mode.

Notebook⇨Define Series

Creates a series for use with the Block⇨Fill command. You can define a series of values or of labels. For example, if you have a large family and you do a lot of scheduling in a notebook, you can define a series with all the names of your family members.

Just the facts

The Define Series dialog box has four buttons along the bottom. The last two are very easy to use. To get rid of a series, select the series and then click on Delete. You get a very polite dialog box asking whether you really want to remove the series. If you're serious, click on Yes, and the series disappears. The Rename button opens a dialog box where you can type a new Series Name and select OK to make the change.

The Create button opens the Create Series dialog box, where you can enter the Series Name and decide upon the Series Type. Your choices for type are List or Formula. If you are creating a list, you have the choice of having each item in the series used only once or of having the list be Repeating. A repeating list can be used to fill a block with more cells than items in the series. If Repeating is not checked and you select a block with more cells than items in the series, the last cells are left blank.

The Modify button opens the Modify Series dialog box. (Just think, someone gets paid for coming up with these dialog box names.) With the Modify Series dialog box, you do not have the option of changing either the series name or type; however, you can change whether a list is Repeating.

The bottom half of both the Create Series and Modify Series dialog boxes works in the same way. What you see there, however, changes — depending upon whether you are working with a list or a formula series.

With a List series, you have the Series Elements section, which contains a list of any values already in the series, and the Value box, where you can enter the text for a new item for the series. You can then select an item already in the series from the list and use the Add button to add the text in Value after the item, the Insert button to put it before the item, or the Modify button to replace the currently selected item with the text in Value. To remove an item from the series, select it from the list and click on the Delete button.

Finally, you can use the Extract button to get values from a block in your notebook. When you select Extract, you get the Extract Values dialog box which you can use to select the block from your notebook. If Override Existing Values is checked, the values from the notebook replace any that were in the list. If this option is cleared, the values are added to the list.

When you are working with a Formula series, the bottom half of the dialog box is the Formula Definition section. You can enter a constant value for use in the series in the Seed Value box. You then can use the Formula box to write a formula for creating the value to put in each cell in the block. Click on the Seed button to insert the value in the Seed Value box. Click on the Previous button to use the value from the preceding cell in the block. Use the Iteration button to include the value representing which cell is currently being filled. The value for Iteration for the first cell in the block is 1; the value is 2 for the second cell, 3 for the third, and so on. It really helps to know a lot of math when creating Formula series.

More stuff

To use the series you defined, you need the Block⊏›Fill or SpeedFill command.

Notebook⊏›Define Style

Notebook⊏›Define Style

Creates a style. A *style* is a combination of formatting that you can apply to a cell or group of cells in a single step. Styles can include information about which font to use, the numeric format, any borders for the cells within the block, and other such information.

Just the facts

You use the same command to create or change a style definition. To change a style, select it from the list under Define Style For. To create a new style, simply type a new name in the box.

The next step is to decide which of the properties listed in the Include Properties section you want to have in your style. (See the tip in the "More stuff" section.) If a property category such as Format or Font is checked, the properties in the style override any settings that were already in place when you apply the new style. If these check boxes are cleared, adding the style does not change these properties. You can always modify the properties after applying the style.

If you have another style that you want to use as a starting point for creating your new style, you can click on the Merge button to load its properties into the dialog box. Simply click on Merge and then select Style in the Merge From section of the Merge Style dialog box. Pick the style you want from the Select Style list and choose OK to load the properties. You can also use Merge to copy the properties from a cell within the current notebook. Click on Merge, select Cell, and then use Select Cell to pick the cell. (You can use the Point Mode button to the left of the box to return to your notebook page to pick the cell.)

To set individual properties, click on the appropriate button (Alignment, Format, Protection, and so on). Each of the buttons represents the same set of properties that are on the Active Block dialog box. For example, the dialog box for the Format properties is the same as the one for the Active Block⇨Format command. Although the dialog boxes may be organized slightly differently, all the settings are the same. Rather than repeat myself more than usual, you can look at these topics for information about setting the properties.

If you want to get rid of a style definition, select it from the Define Style For list box and then click on Delete.

More stuff

One approach, and my favorite, to organizing your styles is to create styles based upon their function. I usually have styles for formatting parts of the page, styles for number formats, and styles to add emphasis.

For example, to format parts of the page, you may have a style for Row Headings and another for Column Headings. These styles usually contain properties for Alignment and Font and may contain information for Text Color and Shading. (You may also include some Line Drawing properties.) Other similar styles may include one for the Table Body or the Totals Row or Column. If you intend to use either the Block⇨Restrict Input command or the Active Block⇨Constraints command, you should also include the Protection property in these styles and create another style called Input Cells, for example, which unprotects cells.

In addition to these styles, create a group that contains only format properties. Finally, create a group that contains styles that add emphasis. These styles include Text Color, Shading, and Line Drawing properties. In general, don't add Font properties as emphasis because they may change the appearance of cells so much that the cells no longer match those around them in the same section.

The most important style in your notebook is Normal — the style that is given to every single cell when you first start out. It is the only style that requires a description for each item in the Included Properties list.

If you just want to change some of the formatting for a cell, you can use such commands as Active Block⇨Font, Active Block⇨Numeric Format, and Active Block⇨Alignment. These commands adjust the same properties that are used for actually setting the styles. You should try to understand these commands before you create your own styles.

Notebook⇨Extract

Takes a block of cells and puts a copy of the block along with any graphs into a new notebook. You have a choice between creating the new notebook with values or actual copies of any formulas in the block.

Just the facts

Selecting Notebook⇨Extract opens the File Extract dialog box. The File Extract dialog box is remarkably similar to the File Save dialog box and includes the Password Protection box for assigning a password. These two dialog boxes do basically the same thing, except that in the File Extract dialog box, you save only a portion of the notebook pages. The cells that you want to put into the new files must be listed in the Block(s) box. You can either select the cells before opening the dialog box or use the Point Mode button to the right of the box to return to your notebook to highlight a block.

You need to decide whether you want the new notebook to contain the formulas that are in the block or just their results. If all the formulas refer to cells in the block you are extracting, you can go ahead and use the Formulas option. If, however, any of the formulas refer to cells that aren't included in the new notebook, you should probably use the Values option. After you make your choice, select OK to create your new notebook.

More stuff

As with the File⇨Save As command, you can use the Save File as Type list on the File Extract dialog box to change the format of the file you are creating. This list enables you to extract a portion of a notebook for use with another program.

To bring information into your notebook, you can use Notebook⇨Combine (from another notebook), Notebook⇨Insert (from another format) or Notebook⇨Text Import (plain text). For more on how to save a file, see File⇨Save As.

Notebook⇨Insert

Brings in information from another file as pages in the current notebook. Only pages that actually contain information are inserted. You can also insert information from other spreadsheet programs.

Just the facts

First, go to the page that you want to have *follow* the pages you are inserting. The inserted pages are then placed *in front of* the current page, and all the remaining pages in the notebook are moved back. Next, choose the Notebook⇨Insert command and select the file you want to insert. You can use the Before Page box to change the page that is to follow the inserted pages. When you select OK, those pages that have something on them are inserted into the current notebook.

More stuff

After you insert some pages in a notebook, the total number of pages in your notebook must be less than 256. If, for example, you are inserting before page AZ and the last page in your notebook that contains anything is page FM, you have 27 pages before the inserted pages and 142 pages that are being used after the insertion. This means that you can insert a maximum of 87 pages. An easier way to figure out how many pages can be inserted is to figure out how many pages are blank at the end of the notebook. In this example, the last page used was FM, which is the 169th page. Just take 256 minus 169 to get the same result of 87 available pages.

If you just want to bring in a text file, use Notebook⇨Text Import. If you want to insert pages from another notebook, you may be better off using Notebook⇨Combine.

Notebook⇨Move Pages

Reorganizes the pages within your notebook. The formulas within the pages remain unchanged.

Just the facts

When you select the Notebook⇨Move Pages command, you get a dialog box where you can identify the page to move (Move Page) and which page you want to insert the page before (To Before Page). By default, the current page is entered in the Move Page box.

More stuff

You can also move pages by clicking on the page tab and dragging the tab to the new location. When you hold down the left mouse button over a tab and start to drag, the cursor changes to an arrow with an attached tab. If you drag the tab out of the window, you create a new view of the page.

Notebook⇨Parse

Breaks a bunch of text into columns. This command is useful if you organized some information as a list within a few cells and now realize that you want each item in its own cell. You usually use this command after you have used Notebook⇨Text Import. If you trust Quattro Pro, you can even combine the two commands by using the Parse Expert option in the Text Import dialog box. Parse is nerd-speak for "break into smaller pieces."

Just the facts

Before using Notebook⇨Parse, make sure that your data is organized so that the Parse command will work. Look at the way the data is put in the cells. Notebook⇨Parse is intended to convert a column of cells into several columns. The information in the first column should consist of several separate entries that have been entered together on a long line. For example, the first column may contain the first name, last name, starting date, age, height, and weight written with spaces separating the items. So one entry may look like the following

```
Stuart    Stuple    06/11/92    29    6'1"    195
```

(Hey, it's my book, I don't have to be honest.) What Parse will do is put each of the items into its own cell.

The second thing you need to look at is whether the spacing within the text will work for parsing. The easiest way to check the spacing is to highlight all the cells containing text and use the Active Block⇨Font command to change the font of the cells to Courier. Courier is what is called a *monospaced font*, which means that each letter is the same width. (*Proportional fonts*, on the other hand, have characters of differing widths. For example, the letter *I* takes up less space than the letter *W*. Most of your fonts are proportional.) The advantage of formatting the text with monospaced fonts is that you can see if the information lines up neatly into columns. In other words, do all the last names start in the same position. If they do, Notebook⇨Parse is the command for you. If they don't, you can either add or remove spaces as necessary to make them line up, or you can try Notebook⇨Text Import.

Next, count how many items are in the text in the first column. In the preceding example, there are six items. Select a block that starts with your first column and extends to the right one column for each item, including the first. In the preceding example, the block would be six columns wide. Extend the block down through all of the rows that contain text. Make sure that all the cells in the block, except for those in the first column, are empty. Now select Notebook⇨Parse.

The way the text is parsed is controlled by what is called a *format line*. A format line uses a series of codes to indicate how Quattro Pro should break the text. The codes used include the ones in the following table:

Code	What It Does
I	Shows at the start of a format line when you are editing it.
V	Marks the start of a value.
L	Marks the start of a label.
T	Marks the start of a recognized time format.
D	Marks the start of a recognized date format.
>	Continues a value, label, time, or date.
*	Appears where there is a space on the sample line but where Quattro Pro thinks a value, label, time, or date continues.
S	Tells Quattro Pro to delete the character in this position when parsing.

Fortunately, you can use the Create button in the Data Parse dialog box. After highlighting the block and opening the dialog box in the preceding example, clicking on the Create button inserts a row containing the following information for the format line:

```
|L>>>>>***L>>>>>***D>>>>>>>>**V>***L>>>***V>>
```

The first L marks the start of the first name, and the greater than symbols (>) indicate that the first name is at least an additional five characters longer. The asterisks (*) indicate that the name can be three characters longer still, up to nine characters in all. The next L starts the last name ,and the symbols show that it, too, can be between six and nine characters long. Notice that Quattro Pro can identify the date (eight characters starting with the D) and recognize the two numbers that can be used as meaningful values (and marks them with a V).

If you understand the parsing codes, you can use the Edit button to open the Edit Parse Line dialog box and make changes to the codes. If you want to have your format line include Ss to deleted characters, you have to add them manually by editing the format line with the Edit button.

Select the OK button to start parsing your lines. Generally, Quattro Pro does enough of the work that you can go through and make minor editing corrections by hand.

More stuff

Whenever possible, use files that contain the columns of information separated by tabs. You can use either File⇨Open or Notebook⇨Text Import to open files with tabs between items. If you can't get tabs, try commas. You can use Notebook⇨Text Import to open files with commas between the items without having to hassle with format lines. Use text files with spaces only as a last resort.

The one situation where Notebook⇨Parse can be a lifesaver is if you are working with an older DOS program. In these programs, the only way to export any of the information may be to have it print to a file on disk.

Another approach for reorganizing text is discussed under Block⇨Reformat. If you trust Quattro Pro to figure out the format line without your help, you can use the Parse Expert option in the Text Import dialog box (which you get by selecting Notebook⇨Text Import) and not bother with all these steps.

<u>N</u>otebook⇨<u>T</u>ext Import

Brings a text file without tabs into the document. You can use this command when you have a list you created in a word processor that you now want to use within a notebook or when you are creating a notebook page with long sections of text. You may need to use <u>N</u>otebook⇨<u>P</u>arse to break the labels into usable columns.

Just the facts

After selecting <u>N</u>otebook⇨<u>T</u>ext Import, you may feel like you got the dialog box from the <u>F</u>ile⇨<u>O</u>pen command by mistake. There is only one difference between the two dialog boxes. That difference, however, is vitally important. In the lower-right corner of the Text Import dialog box is the Option section. It's here that you tell Quattro Pro about the file you are trying to import.

If you select the <u>A</u>SCII Text File option, Quattro Pro reads the file into the first column of the current notebook page. It moves to a new row only when it encounters the combination of a carriage return and a new line. Most DOS and Windows word processors put this combination at the end of each paragraph. ASCII text files usually have this combination at the end of each paragraph, too. One way to check is to open a file using the Notepad utility within Windows. Notepad breaks paragraphs where this combination appears. If you want your text split into multiple columns, you need to use one of the other options.

The difference between the <u>C</u>omma and " Delimited File option and the <u>O</u>nly Comma option is how the options handle the combination of a quotation mark and commas. If your file contains items which themselves contain commas, and you want to put the items into a single column, the items need to be enclosed in quotes. In other words, if you want Stuple, Stuart to appear in a single cell, your text file would need to include something like 29, "Stuple, Stuart", bananas. With the <u>C</u>omma and " Delimited File option, you would get three fields. The first would contain 29, the second would have Stuple, Stuart, and the third would have bananas. If you used the <u>O</u>nly Comma option, you would get four fields. The first would still contain 29, but the second would have "Stuple and the third would have Stuart". The fourth and final cell would contain bananas.

The <u>P</u>arse Expert option reads in a text file and runs the Notebook⇨<u>P</u>arse command in one step. I'm not about to try to explain all of this again, so you have to look under Notebook⇨<u>P</u>arse for an explanation of parsing.

More stuff

When transferring information from another program into Quattro Pro, the best choice is to save the information in a Quattro Pro format from within the other program. The second choice is to save it in a format that Quattro Pro recognizes. (Check the List Files of <u>T</u>ype box on the <u>F</u>ile⇨<u>O</u>pen dialog box for a list.) With both of these options, you can open the file with <u>F</u>ile⇨<u>O</u>pen. The third choice is to save the information with commas between each of the columns (or fields) of information, and the fourth choice is to put commas between the columns. You can open files of these types with <u>N</u>otebook⇨<u>T</u>ext Import. The least preferred solution is to just put spaces between the items so that the columns of text all start in the same position, import it with <u>N</u>otebook⇨<u>T</u>ext Import, and then break it back into columns with <u>N</u>otebook⇨<u>P</u>arse.

You can also bring information into the notebook by using Notebook⇨<u>C</u>ombine (for pages from another notebook) or Notebook⇨<u>I</u>nsert for other files. If you have a text file organized with tabs, you can use either <u>F</u>ile⇨<u>O</u>pen to put it into its own notebook or <u>F</u>ile⇨<u>I</u>nsert to add it to another notebook.

Notebook⇨Update Links

Manages the communication between the current notebook and any *linked* notebook. You create a link (and a linked notebook) whenever you create a formula that references information in a notebook other than the current one. You can create a link if you have a single notebook with product information and separate notebooks for each client. <u>N</u>otebook⇨<u>U</u>pdate Links controls when and how Quattro Pro changes the information in the current notebook based upon what's in the linked notebook.

For mouse maniacs

The Open Links button appears only on the Modeling SpeedBar.

The other links button, Refresh Links, also appears only on the Modeling SpeedBar.

Just the facts

Selecting Notebook⇨Update Links displays a submenu with four choices. The first choice, Open Links, gives you a dialog box where you can open any notebooks that are referenced by links in the current notebook. You are most likely to use this option when you are trying to track down a problem with one of your formulas. If you just want to update the values of your linked formulas by using any changed values from the linked notebooks, you can select the second choice, Refresh Links. Refresh Links goes out and gets the current information from the linked notebooks without having to open them.

You use the third option, Change Links, to move the links from referencing one notebook to referencing another. There are three situations in which this option can be useful. One situation exists when you have two notebooks (one for your own set of finances, for example, and the other for the IRS) that are organized in exactly the same way but which contain different values. In this case, the formulas referencing the linked notebook can contain actual cell references because the same cell address in the two notebooks contains the same information. The second situation exists when you've used named blocks in the formulas that are linked. In this case, it doesn't matter how the notebooks are organized as long as the blocks have the same name. The final situation exists when, for some reason, you've changed the name of the linked notebook. In that case, you have to use Change Links to tell Quattro Pro the location of the information.

The final option, Delete Links, gets rid of any links between the current notebook and the linked notebook. The problem is that the linked formulas are simply replaced with the ERR message. Generally, it's better to replace the linked formulas with their results, either manually or by using Block⇨Values.

Property ⇨ *Object*

Property is a list on the Property Band which gives you access to all the commands that the programmers didn't bother to put on a menu. Quattro Pro also refers to this as the Property Inspector because it lets you work with the dialog boxes used to set the properties of objects. These properties are like commands and include almost all the formatting commands as well as the commands for designing graphs and slides. Many buttons and lists on the Property Band actually make changes to the object's property information. In general, it's a lot easier to use the button or list, unless you are making a great many changes.

Just the facts

Although the Property list on the Property Band does give you an entry for each object currently selected or available, the list doesn't always include what you're looking for. And some of the entries on the list, such as Current Object, are a bit difficult to identify. An easier way to get to an object's Property dialog box is to click on the object with the right mouse button. This action either immediately displays the Property dialog box, or it displays a pop-up menu with a Properties choice as the first item. If you get the pop-up menu, the item's name will change depending on the type of object selected.

The Property dialog boxes generally work in the same way. There is a list of categories along the left side of the dialog box. After you select one of these categories (either by clicking on it or by using the Page Up or Page Down key), the rest of the dialog box changes to show the options within that category. You can make any changes you want and then select another category to change or select OK to have your changes take affect. If you make changes in one category and move on to another category in the same dialog box, the name of the category where you made the changes is displayed in blue.

More stuff

The options on the Property dialog boxes that appear immediately (without the pop-up menu) are discussed under their dialog box titles (Active Page, Active Notebook, and Application). Properties for blocks of cells are discussed under Active Block which is the name of the dialog box even though the command on the pop-up menu is Block Properties. The Properties dialog box associated with graphs is discussed under Graphics⇨Edit Graph. Other Property dialog boxes are discussed with their associated command. There are, however, a great many Property dialog boxes in Quattro Pro, and I'm sure I missed a few. If you're at a loss as to what to do next, try clicking the right mouse button on the object and seeing what options are available through the Properties choice.

The common properties are discussed under their object names. These include Active Block, Active Notebook, Active Page, and Application. Some other objects have their own properties, which are reasonably self-explanatory. (Translation: I didn't have enough room to explain ALL the variants of this super-complex command.)

Slide Show⇨Edit Slide

Despite the name change, this is the same command as
Graphics⇨Edit Slide Show, so that's where I wrote about the
command. After you've started editing, you'll need to use
Property⇨*Object* (the Property Inspector) to make your changes.
To edit the order of the slides, use Slide Show⇨Edit Slide Show
(or Graphics⇨Edit Slide Show).

Slide Show⇨Edit Slide Show

For a better explanation, see Graphics⇨Edit Slide Show. It's the
same command — and Graphics came first.

Slide Show⇨Graph Gallery

See Graphics⇨Graph Gallery. Trust me! It's the same command.

Slide Show⇨Insert Slide

Gives you a dialog box where you can select an existing graph to
use as a slide. You can then set the slide's properties, such as the
transition from the preceding slide, the delay, and whether to use
the master slide.

For mouse maniacs

`Use Master ▼` The Use Master Slide list controls whether the background from
the master slide is used for the current slide.

`No Overlay ▼` The Overlay Previous Slide list lets you keep the preceding slide
on-screen and adds the current slide on top of it.

`Wipe right ▼`

The Effect list sets the transition from the preceding to the
current slide.

`Fast ▼` The Speed list controls the speed of the transition.

`0.5 min ▼` The Display Time list controls how long the current slide is
displayed.

`Show Slide ▼` The Show/Skip Slide list lets you skip over slides that you want in
the slide show as notes to yourself not as slides to be displayed.

Just the facts

If you have a slide selected when you use the Slide Show➪Insert Slide command, the selected slide and all the following slides are moved down one position to make room for the inserted slide. If you don't have a slide selected, the slide is tacked on to the end of the slide show. After selecting the command, you can choose the graph to be inserted as a slide from the aptly named Select Graph for New Slide dialog box. Either double-click on the graph's name or click on it once and then select OK to create the slide.

After you've inserted the slide, the fun part begins. The Property Band now contains lists for setting the transitions between slides in the slide show. The first list, Use Master Slide, determines whether the master slide (shown as the first slide in the film strip) should be used as the background for the current slide. For more information on setting the master slide, see Slide Show➪Master Slide Gallery. The second list, Overlay Previous Slide, controls whether the preceding slide remains on-screen while the current slide is put on top of it.

The next two lists, Effect and Speed, control the transition between the preceding slide and the current slide. There are over 40 different effects available and 3 speeds (slow, medium, and fast). The best way to see how each effect works at the different speeds is to create two slides and try each of the effects. I suggest making two blank slides and giving one of them a colored background (see the tip under "More stuff"). To see the effect, you must use the Slide Show➪Run Slide Show command. If you leave Display Time set to 0.0, just click to move between the slides.

The next list, Display Time, lets you control how long the current slide is displayed before moving to the next slide. If Display Time is set to 0.0 when the slide show is running, you have to click on the current slide to move to the next.

The final slide show list, Show/Skip Slide, controls whether you bother showing the current slide or not. If you select Skip Slide, all the other settings are ignored. (The last two lists on the Property Band, Toolbars and Property, never change.)

More stuff

To create a sample slide, use Slide Show➪New Slide to create a slide without bothering to fill in any of the boxes and then use Slide Show➪Edit Slide to open the slide to work on. Next, click once with the right mouse button and select Type to change the graph to Blank. Finally, select a color set from the third list on the Property Band to color the background.

If you want to reorganize the slides, use Slide Show⇨Edit Slide Show. To create a new slide, use Slide Show⇨New Slide or create it from the notebook as a graph by using Graphics⇨New Graph and then insert it with Slide Show⇨Insert Slide.

Slide Show⇨Master Slide Gallery

Reveals the vast selection of backgrounds that have been created for your "sliding" pleasure. Even more useful is the fact that this command gives you access to the Advisor, which can help you create a presentation that won't embarrass your mother. (Hi, Mom!) The master slide is used to provide a common background for the slides in your show.

Just the facts

The Master Slide Gallery is almost as cool a feature as the Graph Gallery. Like the Graph Gallery, the Master Slide Gallery also has an Advisor feature, which is even cooler than the one for graphs. When you first select Slide Show⇨Master Slide Gallery, the dialog box you see seems rather boring. On the left side of the dialog box are four sample slides, each of which shows a bulleted list. Choose one of these samples to format the image on the right. The image on the right includes any formatting or text from your current master slide. You can use the scroll bar in the middle of the dialog box to see additional master slide samples. The image shown on the right is the background for any slide that uses the master slide. The formatting for the bullets in the selected slide on the left is used for any bulleted slide that uses the master slide as its background.

I already mentioned that the really neat part of this command is the Background Advisor for formatting your master slide. To get to the Advisor, simply click on the Advisor button to reveal this dialog box.

Background Advisor	
Constraints	**Suggestions**
Informal ◄ ► Formal	
Entertaining ◄ ► Serious	
Sophisticated ◄ ► Simple	
Vivid ◄ ► Subdued	
Plain ◄ ► Fancy	
☒ Onscreen ☐ B+W Paper ☐ B+W Trans.	
☐ 35mm Slide ☐ Color Paper ☐ Color Trans.	
☐ Darkened Room ☐ Light Room	
Apply Cancel	Advise Help

As with the Graph Advisor, there are slider bars that let you select the characteristics of your presentation. In addition, there are check boxes to indicate the format of your presentation and the room's lighting conditions. For large screen presentations, your projection choices include Onscreen (for a very large monitor) or 35mm Slide (actually, you'll need more than one). For smaller screen presentations, your projection choices are black-and-white transparencies (B+W Trans.) or color transparencies (Color Trans.). For handouts, your choices are black printing on white paper (B+W Paper) or color printing (Color Paper). If you select any of the projection options, be sure to indicate whether you will be showing the material in a Darkened Room, a Light Room, or normal lighting (neither box is checked).

The slider bar choices on the Background Advisor are much more subjective than those on the Graph Advisor. Your first choice is between an Informal look or a Formal presentation. Your next choice is between a presentation which is Entertaining or one that sets a more Serious tone. The third choice is between a Sophisticated look or a more Simple approach. Your next two choices are whether you want your presentation to be Vivid or Subdued and whether you want a Plain or Fancy format.

After you've set the slider bars, select the Advise button to see the Background Advisor's Suggestions. Although only four sample slides show at one time, there are usually quite a number of suggestions. Simply use the scroll bar at the left of the dialog box to see the other sample slides. You can use one of the recommendations by selecting it and then choosing OK, or you can make changes to the dialog box's settings and select Advise to see another set of Suggestions.

More stuff

You may select any combination of these presentation formats, but you'll get the best results if you select only one of the projection choices, only one of the paper choices, or one of each. The highest quality presentation would use either 35mm slides and color printing or a large screen display (Onscreen) and color printing. A more reasonable approach would be any of the color project choices with black printing on white paper. The budget approach is black-and-white transparencies and black printing on white paper.

Although Quattro Pro shows the master slide samples as bulleted lists, it's generally best to use a blank slide for your master slide. Otherwise, the text on the master slide appears on each and every slide in your slide show. (Well, at least those that use the master slide for a background.) To get a blank master slide, create a master slide by using §lide Show⇨New M§aster Slide. Don't bother filling in any of the boxes — just select OK. Using this technique creates a bulleted list on the slide with placeholder text for each of the items. Now select §lide Show⇨§Edit Slide to edit the graph on the slide. Click once on the graph's background with the right mouse button and then select Type from the pop-up list. Use the dialog box to set the type to B§lank and then select OK. Close the window where you were editing the slide, and you should have a blank slide in the first position on the film strip.

To create a new master slide, use §lide Show⇨New M§aster Slide. The mechanics of using the master slide and transitions are discussed under §lide Show⇨§Insert Slide.

§lide Show⇨New M§aster Slide

Creates a master slide or moves the selected slide to the master slide. The master slide is the slide that appears in the first position of the filmstrip. You can share the background of the master slide with any other slide in the show.

Just the facts

Selecting §lide Show⇨New M§aster Slide creates a new bulleted slide and puts it in the master slide position. Why this command doesn't create a blank slide, I'll never know, but it doesn't. You should click on the new slide and then select §lide Show⇨§Edit Slide. You can now click the right mouse button, select Type from the pop-up menu, select B§lank, and then click on OK. You then want to format the slide by using either §lide Show⇨§Master Slide Gallery or by using the drawing tools on the Graph SpeedBar.

More stuff

To see the gallery of existing masters, use §lide Show⇨§Master Slide Gallery. The mechanics of using the master slide and transitions are discussed under §lide Show⇨§Insert Slide.

§lide Show⇨§New Slide

Creates a new slide and inserts it into the slide show. It's generally easier, however, to go to your notebook page and use §Graphics⇨§New Graph.

For mouse maniacs

Inserts a new slide into the slide show without bothering with the dialog box. Using this button usually results in a blank slide.

Just the facts

This command is like the Graphics⇨New Graph command on a bad hair day. Instead of letting you highlight the block of cells and then create the graph, you are forced to use the Graph Series dialog box to select the blocks that make up the graph. For more information on using this dialog box, you need to look at Graphics⇨Series.

More stuff

It's really much easier to go to your notebook page, highlight the block, use Graphics⇨New Graph, return to your slide show window, and then use Slide Show⇨Insert Slide. OK, I admit that these steps don't sound like they're easier, but if you create a new slide in this way, Quattro Pro does all the work of figuring out which blocks go into which boxes in the Graph Series dialog box.

If you have an existing slide that you want to add to a slide show, you can use Slide Show⇨Insert Slide. If you need an entirely new slide show, use Slide Show⇨New Slide Show. It's often easier to create a new slide if you return to the notebook and create the graph by using Graphics⇨New Graph and then place the graph onto a slide by using Slide Show⇨Insert Slide.

Slide Show⇨New Slide Show

Go directly to Graphics⇨New Slide Show. Do not pass Go. Do not collect $200.

Slide Show⇨Run Slide Show

This is the command that makes using slides worthwhile, and it is explained under its other name: Graphics⇨Run Slide Show.

$\underline{S}$lide Show$\Rightarrow\underline{V}$iew Slide

Shows you the slide, the whole slide, and nothing but the slide. This is the way the slide looks when it is displayed in an on-screen slide show.

For keyboard krazies

Just the facts

Selecting $\underline{S}$lide Show$\Rightarrow\underline{V}$iew Slide causes the slide to be expanded until it takes up the full screen. If you ran the slide show on your computer, your slides would appear the way they do with this command. To return the slide to its previous size, click once with the left mouse button or press Escape.

More stuff

Use the commands on the $\underline{V}$iew menu (such as $\underline{V}$iew$\Rightarrow\underline{L}$arge Slides) for an overview of the entire slide show. To see how a graph looks in various formats, double-click on the graph on the Objects Page and then use the commands on the $\underline{V}$iew menu (such as $\underline{V}$iew$\Rightarrow\underline{3}$5mm Slide).

SpeedBars

Quattro Pro is a bit inconsistent with this term. Although the various long skinny things with buttons across the top of your screen are called SpeedBars in the documentation and in the Help files, the list you use on the Property Band to select between them is called the Toolbar list. So, if you're looking for an explanation of how to switch between SpeedBars, look under the entry for Toolbars.

SpeedFill

Fills the selected block with values based upon the information in the first two cells of the block (those in the upper-left corner). You can fill a block with numbers, dates, days of the week, or any other defined series. This command is only available when you are working with a block on your notebook page and you click the right button or as a button on the Main and Block SpeedBars.

For mouse maniacs

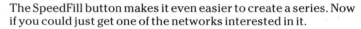

The SpeedFill button makes it even easier to create a series. Now if you could just get one of the networks interested in it.

Just the facts

To use SpeedFill, you need to first enter the starting items in your series in the first few cells of the block you want to fill. SpeedFill uses these items to determine what series to put into the block. For example, if you enter 1 in the first cell and 2 in the second, SpeedFill uses the series 1, 2, 3, 4, and so on. If, however, you entered 1 and 3 in the first two cells, SpeedFill uses the series 1, 3, 5, 7, and so on. SpeedFill recognizes most series of values and any series of labels that has been stored by using the Notebook⇨Define Series command.

You can use either the SpeedFill button or the pop-up menu. For either technique, you need to first enter your values and then select the block you want to fill.

If you want to use a menu, click the right mouse button (while the cursor is over the selection). You see a nifty pop-up menu where you can select the SpeedFill command. The cells in your block are instantly filled with values.

If you want to use the button, just enter your starting values, select the block, and click on the button. Again, the values appear throughout the block.

More stuff

When filling with a series of values, Quattro Pro always tries to find a constant value to add to the preceding value to get the value for the current cell. This is called a *linear* series. If you need to enter a series based upon a more complex mathematical formula, you have two choices. The first is to use Block⇨Fill and define either a power or a growth series. The alternative is to use Notebook⇨Define Series to create a series for SpeedFill to use.

 For more control over the series you want to create, use
Block⇨Fill. The many series used by SpeedFill are defined by
using Notebook⇨Define Series.

SpeedFormat

 Offers a predefined set of formats for the currently selected block.
All the formats provide the option of changing the font, borders,
and shading, but you can decide which elements you use. This
command is only available when you are working with a block on
your notebook page and you click the right button or as a button
on the Main and Block SpeedBars.

For mouse maniacs

 Through the wonders of modern technology, the SpeedFormat
button provides an interior decorator for your notebook.

Just the facts

 If you want to use the pop-up menu, first select the block and
then click the right mouse button (while the cursor is over the
selection). You see a nifty pop-up menu where you can select the
SpeedFormat command. To use the SpeedFormat button, select
your block and then click the button.

In the SpeedFormat dialog box, the Formats list to the left
contains a whole bunch of possible formats. To preview the
formats, simply click on the name and look at the box to the right
(conveniently labeled Example). After you find a format that you
like, you still have some decisions to make in the Include section
at the bottom of the screen. As you change the options in the
Include area, the Example changes to show what formatting has
been applied.

The Include section is divided into two portions: representing
properties and parts of the block. On the left is a list of properties
that you can have SpeedFormat automatically apply. If the check
box next to a property is checked, SpeedFormat uses the settings
for the selected format (from the Formats list). Any settings for
that property that already existed in the block are replaced. If, on
the other hand, the check box is cleared, SpeedFormat ignores
that property and leaves alone any settings you applied.

Most of the properties have the same name in the SpeedFormat dialog box as they do in the Active Block dialog box. For more information, look under that property's name in the Active Block section. For example, for more on the Font property, see Active Block⇨Font. Numeric Format is discussed under Active Block⇨Format. Set Auto-Width is discussed under Active Block⇨Column Width and causes each column in the block to be adjusted to the width of the largest entry in the selected portion of that column. The key word is *selected*. Be careful with this feature — if you haven't selected the entire column, you may find that some of your entries outside the block are cut off.

The options to the right of the Include section control which part of the block SpeedFormat will change. Column Heading determines whether the first row is formatted. Column Total controls the formatting for the last row. Row Heading and Row Total control the first and last column of the block, respectively.

You can also create your own formats for the Format list. First, create a sample block with column and row headings and totals along the right and bottom. Then, format the block by using any of the properties commands. After you have the block looking the way you want, highlight it, select SpeedFormat, and click on the Add button. Give your format a name and click on OK. You may want to experiment with turning on and off the options in the Include section to see how Quattro Pro interpreted your formatting.

To get rid of a format, simply select it from the list and choose Delete.

More stuff

If you don't select a block before starting SpeedFormat, the current block surrounded by blank cells is automatically selected.

If you are planning on printing your notebook, you probably want to turn off the Shading and Text Color properties when using the SpeedFormat dialog box. The only time you wouldn't turn these off is if you happen to have a very nice color printer that can actually make your printed pages as pretty as what you see on-screen.

For a speedy introduction to SpeedFormat, see Chapter 12 in *Quattro Pro 6 For Windows For Dummies*.

To format items by hand, use the styles (discussed under Notebook⇨Define Style) or the specific commands discussed under Active Block (such as Active Block⇨Font and Active Block⇨Line Drawing).

SpeedSum

Creates a formula for adding the contents of a block of cells. This is a particularly strange command because it only exists as a button.

For mouse maniacs

Either select the cell that is supposed to contain the total and have SpeedSum put the formula there or select the block of values and click the SpeedSum button to add an adjacent row or column of numbers.

Just the facts

There are several ways that you can select the cells that will contain the totals. Of course, the easiest way is to click at the bottom of a block contained within a single column. SpeedSum creates a formula by using the @Sum() function to add the contents of all the cells between the formula and the first blank cell above the formula. You can do the same thing with a block contained in a single row by clicking in the empty cell to the right of the block.

You can calculate the totals for all the columns in a block by selecting the cells in the blank row immediately below the block and using SpeedSum. Likewise, you can total the values in the rows of a block by selecting the block of blank cells in the column to the right of the values and using SpeedSum. In fact, you can do both by selecting the block of values plus the additional cells in the blank row below and those in the blank column to the right. SpeedSum totals both the rows and the columns and puts a grand total (the sum of all the values in the block) into the cell at the lower-right corner.

More stuff

For helping in building more complex formulas, use Tools⇨Formula Composer.

Toolbars

Determines which of the SpeedBars is showing. A SpeedBar is a collection of buttons that represents various menu commands. The SpeedBars that are available may change depending upon what you are doing within your notebook. For example, there are special SpeedBars that are available only when you are on the Objects Page or when you are editing a graph or slide show.

For mouse maniacs

 The Toolbar list on the Property Band is used to select which SpeedBar to display.

Just the facts

The SpeedBars provide you with buttons for many of the most useful menu commands. Use the Toolbar list on the Property Band to change which SpeedBar is being displayed. To use one of the commands represented on the SpeedBar, just click on the button.

The various toolbars and the commands associated with each button are discussed in the section of this book called "A Toolbar Tour." The Help information provided by Quattro Pro for SpeedBars is discussed under Help⇨*Identify Button or List*.

More stuff

Which SpeedBars are available on the list depends on what type of window you are working with. If you are on a notebook page, your choices are Main, Block, Format, Draw, and Modeling. If you have a graph window open (which is what you get when you select Graphics⇨Edit Graph), your choices are Graph, Palette, and Align. If you're editing a slide show, your only choice is Slides. The choices on the Property Band stay the same except for the third list, which changes from Styles (when working with a page) to Color sets (when working with a graph), and the fourth list, which changes from Alignment to Legend Position.

 For that mandatory screen tour, see Chapter 3 in *Quattro Pro 6 For Windows For Dummies*. To find out why Quattro Pro insists upon using both Toolbars and SpeedBars to refer to the same thing, see Chapter 6.

To build your own SpeedBars, use Tools⇨Toolbar Designer.

Tools⇨Align

Arranges objects on a graph. The menu command and the object alignment buttons appear only when you are editing a graph.

For mouse maniacs

The Align Left button moves the selected objects so that their left edges are on a line.

The Align Right button moves the selected objects to line up their right edges.

The Align Top button moves the objects so that their tops line up.

The Align Bottom button moves the selected objects so that they are all resting on the same (invisible) line.

The Horizontal Center button moves the selected objects side-to-side so that their centers fall along the same (invisible) vertical line without changing their vertical (up-and-down) placement.

The Vertical Center button moves the selected objects up and down to line up their centers without changing their vertical (side-to-side) placement.

The Vertical Space button takes the selected objects and spreads them out evenly from top to bottom by using a distance you specify.

The Horizontal Space button moves the selected objects so that they are evenly arranged across the graph by using the distance you select.

Just the facts

Although you can use the Align commands to position almost anything within the graph window, the commands are really intended to work with objects that you've drawn on your graph by using the Graph SpeedBar.

The first thing you need to do is to select an object or objects. If you select a single drawn object that has been created automatically with a Graphics command (such as the graph itself or a title), your only choice is to center the object within the graph. (To select a single object, click on it once.) If you want the object in the middle of the graph, select both Vertical Center and Horizontal Center. (The order in which you select these options doesn't matter.) Vertical Center controls the up-and-down placement, and Horizontal Center controls the side-to-side placement.

If you select more than one object (by clicking on the first object and then holding down the Shift key while clicking on other objects), you can use any of the commands to position the items *relative to each other,* which means that the command moves both objects so that they line up. For example, if you select Toolbar⇨Align⇨Left (or use the Align Left button), the objects are moved so that their left edges are along a straight line. The only exceptions to this rule are the Horizontal Space and Vertical Space commands. They both give you a dialog box where you enter a distance value and select OK. The objects are then arranged so that they are evenly spaced using that distance between each pair of objects.

More stuff

You can also select a group of objects by drawing a *selection marquee* around the group. A selection marquee, or just marquee, shows on-screen as a rectangle drawn with a dashed line. Any object that is totally within the rectangle is selected. To draw a marquee, start at the corner where you want one corner of the marquee's rectangle, hold down the mouse button, and drag to the opposite corner. When you release the button, all objects that are completely within the marquee's border are selected.

To remove an item from a group, hold down the Shift key and click on the item.

Objects that have been grouped (using Tools⇨Group) are treated as though they were a single object. The group is indicated by the *handles* that appear around the group. (The handles are the eight small black squares that surround the shape. Dragging a handle changes the object's shape.) The rectangle formed by the handles is what is used for all alignment commands.

To link a bunch of objects so that they move together, use Tools⇨Group. For a quick introduction to the drawing tools on the Graph SpeedBar, see the Graph SpeedBar in "The Toolbar Tour" section.

Tools⇨Consolidator

Takes a set of separate blocks and combines them into a single block. The new block can be created so that it contains either values or formulas. When you combine the separate blocks, you specify whether there are labels to use for grouping the values and what function should be used when combining. (@Sum is the usual choice, but many others are available.)

For mouse maniacs

The Consolidator button is available on the Modeling toolbar.

Just the facts

Well, the best way to use the Consolidator is through the Help⇨Expert⇨Consolidate command, but if you insist upon going it alone with the Tools⇨Consolidator command, here are the basics. In the Consolidation dialog box, the first thing you need to do is pick some Source Blocks by using the Add button. The Source Blocks contain the values to be combined in the *consolidation*, a big word for putting a bunch of things together into a smaller package. You can use the Browse button to add Source Blocks from other notebooks.

If your Source Blocks contain labels, be sure to check either Use Labels in Top Row or Use Labels in Left Column. If you want Quattro Pro to combine the values based upon the labels, the matching labels must run in the same direction. In other words, Quattro Pro can match only labels in the left column of one block with labels in the left column of another block. Quattro Pro can match separate top and left labels for a series of blocks. In other words, if you have color labels in the left column and flower names in the top row for all your blocks, Quattro Pro deals with each color of flower separately. Select the Remove button to get rid of a source block. If you do not use labels, Quattro Pro combines the blocks based upon position.

You also need to select a Destination Block, which is the upper-left corner of where you want the new block to be placed. You can decide whether you want the new block to contain formulas (Output with Formulas is checked) or just values (Output with Formulas is cleared). Finally, select the function to be used on the values for matching cells when combining the blocks.

To perform the consolidation, select Consolidate. To store the settings for later use, select Save As to add it to the list of Consolidations. To delete an entry from the list of Consolidations, select it from the list and select Delete. Select Done to leave the Consolidation dialog box.

More stuff

For simpler operations, you can use Notebook⇨Combine.

Tools⇨*Data Modeling Desktop*

Opens a separate program that creates report tables that summarize your information and then places those reports into a notebook. The program has its own menus and SpeedBars. The reports are based on a crosstab format with subcategories (see "Just the facts" for more information).

For mouse maniacs

The Data Modeling Desktop button takes you from Quattro Pro into its own separate program.

Just the facts

A *crosstab report* is one where the columns and rows are broken into subcategories, each with its own set of calculations. For example, suppose that you have a bunch of information about sales from a variety of locations across the U.S. for the past year.

In a crosstab report, you can list the sales information with a
single city on each row grouped by region and state. For each
region, you can print both the total sales and the average sale for
that region. For the state, you can have the average sales, the
standard deviation for the sales within that state, and the total
sales for the state. Of course, you can also have a grand total of
all of the sales for the entire report. You also can break down the
columns into quarters and calculate averages for each quarter as
well as the yearly average and total.

You can go through your notebook and sort all the cities into the
right order, add the necessary headings, insert some blank rows
and columns, and then create all the formulas to do the calculations — but the Data Modeling Desktop can do all these steps for
you. The Data Modeling Desktop is a separate program that takes
information from your notebook and organizes it as a crosstab
report. You can then return the report to your current notebook
or to another notebook.

The advantage to using the Data Modeling Desktop is that it does
most of the work for you and makes it much easier to change
your mind. The disadvantage is that it is a separate program and
requires you to invest time and energy to learn it.

Although it is not a terribly difficult program to learn, it has many
more options than can be described here. (Translation: You're on
your own for this one.) The Data Modeling Desktop does have its
own Help system, however. To get there, either start the Data
Modeling Desktop program and select Help or search Quattro
Pro's Help for information on the Data Modeling Desktop command.

Tools⇨Database Desktop

This one must be complex — it comes with its own manual! This
is a separate Database program worthy of its own Quick Reference.

For mouse maniacs

The Data Desktop button on the Modeling SpeedBar gives you
instant access to the Database Desktop program.

Just the facts

The Database Desktop is a relational database that is designed for
use with a wide variety of products, including Quattro Pro. You
can use the Database Desktop to create your own databases,
design queries within those databases, and use the information
from the Database Desktop in Quattro Pro.

More stuff

You can use a database from the Database Desktop as the source of data to use with the Tools⇨Database Tools command.

Tools⇨Database Tools

Enables you to work with a set of rows and columns as a database. Each column must contain a field name at the top and the entries for the field within the column. Each row is a record within the database. You can use the Table Query, Link Table, and Aliases commands to maintain a relationship with an *external database* (a database managed by another program), but they are not discussed in this reference.

For mouse maniacs

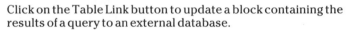

Click on the Table Link button to update a block containing the results of a query to an external database.

Just the facts

The first two commands on the Tools⇨Database Tools menu are designed for working with small databases contained within your Quattro Pro notebook pages. A database is just a list of information organized so that each column contains the same category of information. To set up a database, decide what fields (or categories) of information you want to include in your list. Then decide on a name for each category. Put these names in a row on one of your database pages with one name in each cell. Do not skip cells. You may want to highlight the columns and click on the Fit button on the Main SpeedBar. For the example in the figure, I used First Name, Last Name, Birthday, and Favorite Flower and put them in cells A1, A2, A3, and A4. Then highlight the names and the empty cells on the row below them and select Tools⇨Database Tools⇨Form. You get something like the first figure shown here.

Filling in all the text boxes creates a single record, and each record is put into its own row. Enter your information for the first row by filling in the text box along the left of the dialog box and then selecting New to store those entries and get a new blank record. If you want, you can leave some of the boxes blank, but you can't put more than one item into each box. You can also enter the information into the blank cells below the field names, but people will be more impressed if you use the form.

To move through the records that you have already entered, use

the scroll bar to the right of the boxes or select the Go Next or Go Previous button. To get rid of a record, move through the records until the one you want to get rid of is displayed in the dialog box and then select Delete. You can change the information in a record by moving to the new record and editing the information in the text boxes. Move to another record (or create one with New) to confirm your changes or click on Revert to restore the original information. You must click on Revert before moving to another record.

You can use the Search button to move to a blank screen where you can enter information to be used for searching for matches. Enter the information you want to match into the appropriate box and then select Go Next to move to the first match. Use Go Next and Go Previous (or the scroll bars) to move between the matching records. To return to the dialog box for adding or editing records, select Edit. When you are finished, select the Close button to return to your notebook.

Although you can do a lot with simple searches, to look for records based upon rules or conditions, you need to create a *query*. A query is simply a question that you are asking the database. The *conditions* are the specific parts of the query phrased so that Quattro Pro understands what you are looking for. A typical query may be to find everyone in the database born before 1/1/65. The condition is "Birthday <= 1/1/65."

To create a query, first copy the field names to two additional pages of your notebook. Next, change the page name for the original page to Database and the other two pages to Criteria and Extract. You now need to create the rules, or conditions, for matching records. (Create the criteria in the same way that you create the criteria for the @If( ) functions described in the section "Fun and Functional Formula.") You can also look through Quattro Pro's Help system for information about creating criteria. After you've set up your three pages (the Extract page has only the field names), select Tools⇨Database Tools⇨Query. See the nice query screen?

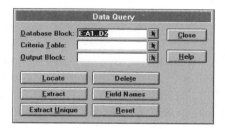

You may notice that the Data Query dialog box has room for three blocks: one for the Database Block, one for the Criteria Table, and one for the Output Block. Select the field names and all the records on your first page for the Database Block. Select the field names and the conditions you've entered as the block for the Criteria Table. Select the field names on the third page (the Extract page) for the Output Block.

Select Locate to have Quattro Pro highlight all the records on your Database page that match the conditions in the criteria. Select Extract to have Quattro Pro copy the matching records to the Extract page. You can rearrange the field names on the Extract page to change the order of the columns. If you want, you can delete field names from the Extract page if you don't want to have the information from that field copied, but you cannot leave gaps between the field names. In other words, don't just clear the cell with the field name you want to get rid of; instead, delete the column. Select Extract Unique to have only those records that are unique copied. This step is useful when you have duplicate records in your list, and you need only one copy of each. Select Delete to get rid of all the records that match the criteria. Reset erases the information in the dialog box but does not change anything in your notebook.

More stuff

It really is easier to simply enter the information into the cells under the field names. Just be careful that you don't skip any rows. You can format the rows and the information by using any of Quattro Pro's normal tools, including the number formats.

If you want to work through an example of using a database, see Chapter 16 in *Quattro Pro 6 For Windows For Dummies*.

Tools⇨*Export Graphics*

Takes a graph that you have created and saves it as a separate file for use by other programs.

Just the facts

To get to this command, you must be working with a graph window (use Graphics⇨Edit Graph). When you select Tools⇨Export Graphics, you get a dialog box that bears a remarkable resemblance to the Save As dialog box because they both perform the same function. Use the Export Graphics File dialog box to select a destination for the file, provide a filename, and choose a file format. Be sure to use a file format recognized by the program you intend to work with.

There is a wide variety of formats available, and your most important consideration is what formats your other program can use. There are a few guidelines, however. In most cases, EPS gives you the highest quality. If you're working with black-and-white images, you can get very good results by selecting TIF. The TIF extension creates files in Tagged Information File Format (TIFF), which can be quite large. If your other program accepts the format, you may want to select PackBits for TIFF Compression (which creates a smaller file). Windows programs can read PCX, BMP, or CGM, all of which are medium quality color formats. With most of the formats, you can elect to translate the graph into shades of gray by selecting Bitmap Gray Scale.

More stuff

The graph window's contents are exported so that the resulting file resembles the graph screen as closely as possible. Be sure to select an appropriate option from the View menu to set the proportions of your graph. For example, if you intend to print your graph on slides, you should select View⇨35mm Slides.

For information about saving notebooks in other formats, see File⇨Save As. To bring graphics into Quattro Pro, use Tools⇨ Import Graphics.

Tools⇨Formula Composer

Guides you through the process of creating your formulas.
Learning to use this tool is generally more efficient than having to
keep a huge pile of junk food available for bribing the office guru.
Of course, there are still some things that require a package of
Tiger Bars. . . .

For mouse maniacs

Click on the Formula Composer button for help in building your
formulas.

When you are editing the contents of a cell, you can use the
Function button to jump to the list of functions contained within
the Formula Composer.

For keyboard krazies

$\boxed{Ctrl} + \boxed{F2}$

Just the facts

Select Tools⇨Formula Composer to open the Formula Composer—
sort of a souped-up calculator. As you can see in the figure, the
left side of the dialog box has an outline of the formula, and the
right side has various tools for creating your formula.

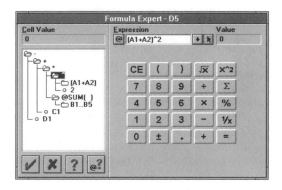

The left side shows your formula with each level marking the priority, as Quattro Pro sees it. Items that are indented furthest are done first, and Quattro Pro works from right to left in calculating the result. Items on the same level are generally calculated from top to bottom. You can click on any folder in the outline to see the calculation or formula for that branch.

When you first open the Formula Composer, the right side of the dialog box has a number of buttons resembling the keys on a calculator. The buttons work in the same manner as calculator keys, except that you need to click on the buttons with the mouse instead of pushing them on-screen with your finger. In fact, you can use the Formula Composer as a quick calculator within Quattro Pro. The only key you may not recognize is the one at the end of the fourth row (counting up from the bottom). It's the one next to the division key. The symbol on the key is the Greek letter sigma, and clicking on this button adds the @Sum() function to your formula. The calculator keypad is displayed whenever a cell reference or simple mathematical operation (add, subtract, multiply, or divide) is selected in the outline to the left.

At the top of the right side are several tools for building your formula. The Point Mode button is used to return to your notebook page to select a block. (Its use is described under Block⇨Copy.) The button with the @ sign on it is used to open the Functions dialog box. This is the same dialog box that you can open from the input line on the notebook page. In fact, it's the same button as the one on the notebook page. (By the way, the button next to it on the input line, which is not available within the Formula Composer, gives you access to Quattro Pro's built-in macros.)

The Functions dialog box is organized by categories that are listed on the left. When you select a category, the right side of the dialog box displays the functions within that group. The first category, All, shows all of Quattro Pro's functions. The next category, Recently Used, shows a list of some of the functions you have used in your notebook. When you select a function from the list on the right, the bottom portion of the dialog box displays a brief description of the function. After you find a function that looks like what you need, double-click on it or select it and then select OK.

When you return to the Formula Composer dialog box, it may take a moment for the outline to update, but after it is complete, the calculator on the right side is replaced with information designed to help you use the function. The bottom portion of the right side may contain boxes for you to enter the various arguments required by the function. All in all, it's a pretty neat way to learn how to create formulas. You can get the same information for any function in your formula by clicking on it in the outline on the left.

The four buttons along the bottom of the left side are symbols representing the normal dialog box controls. The green check mark is the same as OK. The red X is Cancel, and the blue question mark is Help. The fourth button with the @ symbol and a blue question mark is designed to give you additional help on the functions.

More stuff

There are a number of tricks for working with the outline view of your formula. If you click with the right button, you get a pop-up menu for expanding and collapsing the outline as well as tracing the various parts of the formula — both within the outline and from your notebook. To move from the formula in the current outline to one that is in a cell being referenced, select the reference and then select Follow from the pop-up menu (or use Ctrl+F). To return to the preceding formula, select Back from the pop-up menu (or use Ctrl+B).

Be very careful with the Value choice from the pop-up menu. It replaces the selected reference with the current value for that reference. Unfortunately, if the reference cell has the wrong value, there's no way to change it or make the reference come back.

If you are having difficulty with remembering how to use a particular function, open the Formula Composer, select the function, and use the Help information to figure out what you need to do.

When you insert a function from the Functions dialog box directly onto the input line, you don't get the Help information that is shown within the Formula Composer. You do, however, get some help. The general, *syntax* for the formula is shown along the bottom of the screen. The syntax is an attempt to mark how the formula is supposed to be put together by using words or short phrases to stand for each block address or value.

Very often, the best way to use the Formula Composer with more involved formulas is to write the formula yourself and then, if you run into difficulty, open the dialog box. There are two major advantages to this approach. First, it's much faster to type the formula into the cell rather than to wait for the Formula Composer to update between your changes. Second, the outline is more complete and more likely to show you your problem.

You can resize the Formula Composer dialog box by dragging any of the outer borders. You can adjust the size of the outline area by dragging the dividing line. Making the dialog box larger makes it easier to see more of the outline, which gives you a better chance for understanding the formula as shown.

For the simplest formula, such as adding up a row or a column, you can use SpeedSum. To create formulas that combine information in separate blocks organized with labels, use Tools⇨Consolidate.

Tools⇨Group

Combines the selected objects into a single group that can be moved as a single unit.

For mouse maniacs

The Group button is available when you are editing a graph.

Just the facts

Select two or more objects and then select Tools⇨Group. The individual handles around the object disappear to be replaced by a single set surrounding the group of objects. This single set of handles indicates that the group can be positioned and sized as through it were a single object. (For information about selecting several objects or working with handles, see the notes in "More stuff".)

More stuff

Probably the easiest way to select more than one object is by clicking on the first object and then holding down the Shift key while clicking on the other objects. You can also select a group of objects by drawing a *selection marquee* around them. To draw a selection marquee, start at the corner where you want the marquee's rectangle to be, hold down the mouse button, and drag to the opposite corner. When you release the button, all objects that are completely within the marquee's border are selected. To remove an item from a group, hold down the Shift key and click on it.

The *handles* around an object or group are the eight small black squares that surround the shape. When the handles are displayed, the object is selected. You can drag a handle to change the object's shape and size. When the cursor is over the handle, it turns into a large plus sign. When the cursor is over the rest of the image, dragging causes the image to move. The rectangle formed by the handles is what is used for all alignment commands.

 To break the group back into independent objects, use Tools➪Ungroup. You usually group objects to change the way they work with Tools➪Align.

Tools ➪ *Import Graphics*

Brings in a graphic created in another program. You may use this command for including your company logo on your graphs.

For mouse maniacs

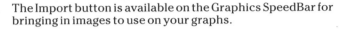 The Import button is available on the Graphics SpeedBar for bringing in images to use on your graphs.

Just the facts

The only difference between the Import Graphics File dialog box and the one for File➪Open is that the List Files of Type box contains extensions for graphic file formats. When you've located the file containing the graphic you want to import, either double-click on its name or select it and click on OK.

The image is placed in the upper-left corner of the graph window. You can use the mouse to drag it to a new location (by dragging from within the figure) or to change the image's size and shape (by dragging on one of the eight handles that surround the object — the cursor resembles a large plus sign when it's in position).

More stuff

Images stored in EPS files cannot be important unless they also contain a bit-mapped version of the image. This bit-mapped image is what Quattro Pro uses for display, and without it, Quattro Pro has no way of manipulating the image.

 You can use the commands on the Tools menu (such as Tools➪Group, Tools➪Align, and Tools➪Object Order) to work with the image as though it were a drawn object.

Tools ➪ *Macro*

Translates instructions that you place on your notebook page into commands for Quattro Pro. You can associate a keystroke or button with these commands so that they can be easily repeated whenever you need them.

Just the facts

To start recording a macro, select Tools⇨Macro⇨Record. You get the Record Macro dialog box, where you must enter a block address as a Location to store the macro or select a name for the macro from the list of Macro/Named Blocks. After you select OK, you can perform the tasks you want recorded in the macro. After the last action you want recorded, select Tools⇨Macro⇨Stop Record.

The setting on the Tools⇨Macro submenu that is likely to give you the most problems is Options, which controls whether the recording is done by using Absolute Reference (where the macro always affects the same cells) or Relative Reference (where the macro starts wherever the cursor is and moves relative to that starting point).

The difference is easy to understand when you create a sample macro that puts your name in one cell, moves down a cell, and puts your address in that cell. Suppose that you use Absolute Reference to record your name in cell B3 (the current cell) on page F. Then you enter the address in cell B4 on page F. Now every time you run the macro, it puts your name in the current cell, moves to cell B4 on page F (where you put your address while recording), and puts your address in that cell. No matter where you start the macro, it moves to cell B4 on page F to insert the address. Not exactly what you want! If you record with Relative Reference, however, when you play the macro, it puts your name in the current cell, moves down one cell on the same page, and puts your address there. No matter where you start the macro, it moves down one cell relative to the current cell.

To have Quattro Pro perform the tasks you recorded, select Tools⇨Macro⇨Play, which lets you select a macro based upon its Location or from the list of Macro/Named Blocks.

Selecting the Tools⇨Macro⇨Debugger command causes a special window to appear the next time you play a macro. This window is filled with strange and nerdy tools for figuring out why the macro isn't working. If your macro doesn't work, it is often easier to do the tasks assigned to the macro by hand rather than to try to fix the macro.

More stuff

To learn what you need to know about Macros, see Chapter 18 in *Quattro Pro 6 For Windows For Dummies*.

Tools⇨Numeric Tools

Displays a submenu with a variety of mathematical, statistical, and analysis tools. These tools are intended for very specialized purposes, which are beyond the scope of this book (and in a few cases, even beyond the scope of the author). Quite frankly, if you don't recognize the names of these tools, then you probably don't need to use them. The tools included are detailed in "Just the facts."

Just the facts

Three commands provide high-powered analysis tools: Analysis Tools, Regression, and What-If. If you are comfortable with the underlying logic for these analysis tools, you can simply select them from the menu. Those of us that prefer to save our brain cells for more important things (such as figuring out the relationships on *Babylon 5*) may prefer to use the commands via Help⇨Experts. The Help⇨Experts⇨Analysis Tools command is a catch-all for a variety of statistical analyses. In the Expert system, the Regression command does not get its own heading, but it is covered under the Analysis Tools command.

The next two commands are for working with matrixes and allow you to Invert a matrix and to Multiply two matrixes. With both commands, you have to enter the blocks containing the starting matrix (or matrixes, if you're multiplying) and the destination. Remember that when you multiply two matrixes, the size of the final matrix is determined by the size and shape of the original two.

The Frequency command searches a block or blocks of cells (the Value Blocks) based upon the values listed in the Bin Block. The values for the Bin Block should be in a single column in increasing order.

The Optimizer is used to find solutions to linear or nonlinear problems with control over the type of solution sought and the constraints upon the problem model. With a tool like this, why don't people do something about world hunger?

The final command, Solve For, takes a reference for a formula within a single cell (the Formula Cell), the address of a single cell referenced by the formula that contains a value that is allowed to change (the Variable Cell), and a desired result (Target Value). The command then uses the formula in the Formula Cell and the target value to calculate the value required in the Variable Cell. You can control the maximum number of times Quattro Pro cycles through a circular reference (Max Iterations) and the minimum level of accuracy acceptable to stop before the maximum of iterations has been reached (Accuracy).

Provides the tools you need for managing the exchange of information across networks by using the Object Exchange (OBEX) system. Not too surprisingly, you only get this command when you install OBEX along with Quattro Pro.

Just the facts

There are three options for the Tools⇨Object Exchange submenu. The first, Manage Pages, displays a dialog box for controlling the updating and version history of inserted pages. The Manage Inserted Pages dialog box displays a list of all pages that have been added to the current notebook with either the File⇨Subscribe or File⇨Send commands. You can change which version of the pages you are using (assuming more than one has been published), change between manual and automatic updating when new pages become available, and rename the inserted pages. You can also force an immediate update or delete the pages.

The second command, Tools⇨Object Exchange⇨Address Book, opens the program for managing your OBEX address book. You can change the aliases, names, and account information for those with whom you share information. Accounts need to be established separately by using the actual Object Exchange program, which can be started from Windows or via the OBEX dialog boxes.

The final command, Tools⇨Object Exchange⇨Poll Now, is certainly not the least because it's the one you are most likely to use. Poll Now causes Quattro Pro to send any messages you have created with the File⇨Send or File⇨Publish commands, check for any new messages in your OBEX account, and check for updates to published pages. You use this command if your network software does not automatically notify you of new messages or changes in the contents of pages to which you have a subscription.

More stuff

The commands for sharing your information or for using other people's information via OBEX are File⇨Publish, File⇨Send and File⇨Subscribe.

Tools⇨Object Order

Controls which objects appear to be on the top of the stack.
Objects on top can cover up parts of those objects beneath them.
Each object exists on its own imaginary layer, which you can
move by using these commands.

For mouse maniacs

The Bring Forward button moves the selected object(s) one layer
closer to the top.

The Send Backward button moves the selected object(s) one
layer further away.

The Bring to Front button brings the selected object(s) to the
very top of the stack.

The Send to Back button throws the selected object(s) all the way
to the bottom of the stack.

Just the facts

For this command, it really helps if you're either working on a
graph or you've created some objects and placed them on your
notebook page. An object can be a graph or any image created by
using the Draw SpeedBar. Each separate object on the page has
its own layer. It may help to think of the objects as being printed
on transparent paper. When an object is on top of the pile, it is
positioned closer to the viewer and can cover up other objects.
The commands on Tools⇨Object Order are used to change the
order of the object layers.

Selecting an object and then choosing the Tools⇨Object
Order⇨Bring to Front command causes that object to jump to the
top of the stack (closest to the viewer). Any other objects in the
same area of the screen are then partially or completely hidden.
Tools⇨Object Order⇨Send to Back causes the selected object to
move to the bottom of the stack (furthest away from the viewer)
where it is partially or completely covered by other objects in the
same area. Bring Forward moves the selected object one layer
closer to the viewer (towards the top of the stack). Selecting an
object and then choosing the Tools⇨Object Order⇨Send Back
command moves the object one layer away from the viewer
(toward the bottom of the stack).

More stuff

 You can also select Object Order from the menu that appears when you click once with the right mouse button while the cursor is within the boundary of an inserted object on a notebook page.

If you have more than one object selected, they are all moved together, and their layers within the selection remain the same.

 If an object is completely hiding another object, the only way to get to the hidden object is by sending the first one further away until it no longer is covering the second object. Often, it is easiest to send the first object all the way to the back (with Send to Back) and then re-arrange the order.

You may need to move an object several times to reveal another object that is being hidden. Imagine that you have four objects — conveniently labeled as Object-1, Object-2, Object-3, and Object-4 — with Object-1 the closest to the viewer and the others in order toward the back (with Object-4 being the furthest from the viewer). Now, part of Object-1 is covering up part of Object-3, and you need to see all of Object-3. You select Object-1 and then select Tools⇨Object Order⇨Send Back. The objects are now — from front to back — Object-2, Object-1, Object-3, and Object-4. Unfortunately, your problem hasn't gone away because Object-1 is still in front of Object-3. Fortunately, selecting Tools⇨Object Order⇨Send Back again (with Object-1 still selected) solves your problem with the objects in order (again from front to back) as Object-2, Object-3, Object-1, and Object-4.

 The easiest way to put a group of controls in order is to select the one you want on top and then send it to the back. Next, select the control to be on the second layer and send it to the back (behind the one you just moved). Continue this process until you've moved all the controls into the order that you want.

Other commands for working with objects include Tools⇨Align, Tools⇨Group and Tools⇨Ungroup.

Tools⇨Scenario Manager

Tracks the changes and the results of these changes in your notebook. This is a very powerful tool for building reports that show the range of possibilities.

For mouse maniacs

Click on the Scenario Manager button to open the Scenario Manager dialog box.

Just the facts

To be frank, the best way to use the Scenario Manager is via Help⇨Experts. Your starting scenario should already be set up, and you need to decide which cells within the scenario have values that will change (the *changing cells*) and which cells have formulas that will be affected by those changes. Scenario Manager then allows you to identify these two groups of cells as the ones of interest, make changes to the values in your changing cells, and track the results of those changes. Scenario Manager generates a report with the changes you made and how the changes affected the results.

More stuff

Use Block⇨Copy to duplicate your model in various locations in your notebook. Scenario Manager can then track and compare the changes you make to the different models.

Tools⇨Spell Check

Checks the spelling of all the words you use within your notebook. This is a long overdue tool for helping accountants look like they read and write English. (Something we authors have editors for!)

Just the facts

After you select Tools⇨Spell Check, you can begin checking the words in your document by clicking on the Start button in the Spell Check dialog box. Quattro Pro starts looking at all the words contained in any of the cells within your notebook. When the program encounters a word that it doesn't recognize, it stops and displays that word as an error. At this point, you get a chance to use all the other buttons on the dialog box.

If the word is correct, you have three options. You can select Skip Once to go on with the spell check. With this option, Quattro Pro stops again if it encounters the same word. You can click on Skip Always to have Quattro Pro skip the word in this case and any other time it encounters it within the notebook. You can use either of these options for a word that you use infrequently but is correct within this notebook. Your third choice for dealing with a correct word is to select A̲dd, which has Quattro Pro insert the word into your own dictionary. You will want to use this option for frequently used words that Quattro Pro does not recognize.

If the word is not correct, Quattro Pro attempts to figure out what you really meant and lists its ideas in the Sugge̲stions box. The word that Quattro Pro thinks is the most likely choice is placed in the Replace W̲ith box. If the word in the Replace W̲ith box is the one you want, great! If not, check through the list and, if you locate the word, click on it once. If you don't locate the word in the list, or Quattro Pro doesn't suggest a word, you need to figure out the proper spelling and type the correct information into the Replace W̲ith box yourself. After the information in the Replace W̲ith box is correct, you can select the Re̲place or R̲eplace All button to have Quattro Pro change the incorrect word to the correct one in the Replace W̲ith box. If you select the Re̲place button, Quattro Pro changes only the selected word. The program stops and asks you again if it finds the same word elsewhere. If you select R̲eplace All, however, Quattro Pro changes the word each time it finds the word, without stopping to ask your permission.

You can use the O̲ptions button to control which, if any, words Quattro Pro skips. The two choices tell Quattro Pro to Ignore Words with N̲umbers and to Ignore U̲PPERCASE Words. A check next to an option tells Quattro Pro to ignore that type of word. If your Windows environment is set up with dictionaries installed for other languages, you can use the L̲anguage list to select a different language dictionary. You can use the C̲hoose New Dictionary button to select a new personal dictionary. You may want to keep separate dictionaries if you use special words occasionally. You can put the unusual words into their own dictionary and load this dictionary only when you need to.

Select C̲lose to stop the spell check before it reaches the end of the notebook.

More stuff

If you start the spell check somewhere other than cell A1 on page A, Quattro Pro checks through the notebook until the last page and then stops and presents a dialog box asking whether it should start from the beginning. If you want to be sure that all the notebook is checked, select Y̲es.

Tools ⇨ *Toolbar Designer*

Enables you to create your very own SpeedBars (toolbars). Of course, you don't have to create your own SpeedBars unless commands that you use often don't appear on the regular SpeedBars or unless you are writing your own macros, and you want to add them to a SpeedBar.

Just the facts

After selecting Tools⇨Toolbar Designer, you are placed in a separate work area with a blank toolbar. You add buttons to the blank toolbar either by using the built-in button collections representing existing Quattro Pro commands or by creating your own buttons for running a macro that you have written.

Use the Buttons list on the Controls SpeedBar to display the various toolbars with the built-in button collections. (The Buttons list is the second from the right. The list on the far right controls which toolbar is currently active.) To copy a button from one of the built-in collections, select the collection and then click on the button you want. Next, move to your toolbar and click where you want the button to be placed. You can use the button outline attached to the cursor to help position the new button.

To add a button to run a macro, draw the button using the Bitmap Button tool (the one with a small box containing a check mark). You can then assign a macro to the button by using Tools⇨Assign Macro. To change the bitmap on the button, click on the button with the right mouse button and then select BitmapButton Properties from the pop-up menu and then Bitmap from the submenu.

To get rid of a button from your toolbar, select the button and press the Delete key.

After you have added all the buttons you want, use the Toolbar⇨Save command to give the toolbar a name and store it in the Quattro Pro directory. Select Toolbar⇨Close All to return to your notebook.

To use your new toolbar, select the Append Toolbar command from the Toolbars list on the Property Band and then use the dialog box to locate the file containing your toolbar. To open the toolbar, click on the Close Toolbar button (the one with the big red X at the right end).

Use Toolbar⇨Open to open an existing custom toolbar and to make changes to it.

More stuff

You can select the Align SpeedBar from the Property Band within the Toolbar Designer to position the buttons on your new toolbar. Selecting several buttons and using the Horizontal Center and Horizontal Space alignment buttons is the most useful technique for creating attractive SpeedBars. To select several buttons, click on the first button and then hold down the Shift key while you click on additional buttons to add to the group. To return to the standard Toolbar Designer tools, select Controls from the Toolbars list.

You can also use the Edit⇨Cut, Edit⇨Copy, and Edit⇨Paste commands (or their SpeedMenu equivalents when you click with the right mouse button) to move buttons between toolbars.

The commands on the File menu within the Toolbar Designer work with notebooks (File⇨Save saves the current notebook). To open, save, or close a toolbar, use the commands on the Toolbar menu.

For information on using toolbars, see the SpeedBar entry. To design a more complex system, use Tools⇨UI Builder.

Tools⇨UI Builder

Gives you all the tools you need to design your own *user interface* components. User interface is a fancy way of describing the parts, such as menus and dialog boxes, that make up a program. This command is pretty hard-core nerd stuff, but you can have fun playing around and designing dialog boxes that don't really do anything.

Just the facts

The fact is that this this command is far too complex to explain in the time we have remaining. (I've always liked that expression) and cannot be easily described. For most purposes, the Toolbar Designer is more likely to meet your needs. If you need the UI Builder, you're probably a C++ programmer and should be writing these books instead of buying them. The UI Builder works very much like the Toolbar Designer, but it has more options.

More stuff

To create your own SpeedBars, use Tools⇨Toolbar Designer.

Tools ⇨ *Ungroup*

Breaks a grouped object back into the original objects that you used to create it. In other words, this command undoes the effect of a Tools⇨Group command.

For mouse maniacs

The Ungroup buttons breaks the selected group back into individual objects.

Just the facts

Click on the grouped object to select it and then select Tools⇨Ungroup. The objects that had been grouped together can now be selected as individual objects. To stop selecting objects, click on any other part of the screen.

More stuff

Each object or grouped object (except lines, which have two) is marked by eight handles after it is selected The handles are represented by small black squares at the four corners and in the middle of each of the four sides. Dragging on a handle resizes the object within the handles. A grouped object has a single set of handles.

You can have a grouped object that itself is made up of several other grouped objects. In this case, when you ungroup the combined objects, each of them is still its own group.

To put objects into a group, use Tools⇨Group. You usually group and ungroup objects to change the way they move when you use Tools⇨Align.

View⇨35mm Slide

Changes the display of the slide to resemble the proportions of a 35mm slide.

Just the facts

All you can do with View⇨35mm Slide is select it and look at the screen. The slide now appears on-screen in the same proportion as it would appear if you printed it as a 35mm slide. When you adjust the size of the window, the graph is shown at the largest possible size that maintains the proportions.

More stuff

For a full screen graphic, use Graphics⇨View Graph. For other sample views, use View⇨Floating Graph, View⇨Full Extent, View⇨Printer Preview or View⇨Screen Slide.

View⇨Display

Provides a dialog box for controlling which parts of the screen are displayed during the current session. Parts of the screen that can be hidden or displayed include the Property Band, SpeedBars, scroll bars, and pretty much everything except the title bar and the menu bar.

Just the facts

Selecting View⇨Display gives you the Display dialog box, which combines settings from Application⇨Display and Active Notebook⇨Display. Making changes to the Display dialog box has the same effect as making changes with either of the other two commands. Because I've already discussed these settings earlier, this is going to be a very short entry. That's it!

More stuff

To learn a bit more about using this command, see Chapter 15 in *Quattro Pro 6 For Windows For Dummies*.

Settings for the same items can also be set by using Active Notebook⇨Display and Application⇨Display.

View⇨Floating Graph

Formats your graph in its graph window with the same proportions that are used when placing it on a notebook page.

Just the facts

All you can do with View⇨Floating Graph is select it and look at the screen. This command is available only if you have inserted the graph somewhere in your notebook first. After you select the command, the graph in the window is proportioned to match the inserted graph. When you adjust the size of the window, the graph is shown at the largest possible size that maintains the same proportions as the one on the notebook page.

More stuff

For a full screen graphic, use Graphics⇨View Graph. For other sample views, use View⇨35mm Slide, View⇨Full Extent, View⇨Printer Preview or View⇨Screen Slide.

View⇨Full Extent

Expands the graph so that its proportions match those of the graph window.

Just the facts

All you can do with View⇨Full Extent is select it and look at the screen. After you select the command, the graph in the window expands to fill the entire window. When you adjust the size of the window, the graph changes to match the new size and proportions of the window.

More stuff

For a full screen graphic, use Graphics⇨View Graph. For other sample views, use View⇨35mm Slide, View⇨Floating Graph, View⇨Printer Preview, or View⇨Screen Slide.

View⇨Group Mode

Changes the page tabs so that you can identify which pages belong to the group and applies any formatting to all the pages within the group.

For keyboard krazies

$$\boxed{Alt} \; + \; \boxed{F5}$$

Just the facts

Selecting View⇨Group Mode lets you take advantage of the groups that you created by using the Notebook⇨Define Group command. The pages within each group are marked with a blue border at the bottom of the page tabs. Any formatting changes made to a page within the group are made to all pages in the group. This feature allows you to give your pages a consistent look. When Group Mode is active, there is a check next to the command on the View menu. When Group Mode is inactive (meaning that you can format pages in the group separately), there is no check.

More stuff

It's generally easier to set up the formatting on your grouped pages first and then turn off Group mode. In this way, you can make individual changes to pages without accidentally causing problems on another page. When you want to format something across the pages, turn Group mode back on.

To create the groups to use, use Notebook⇨Define Group.

View⇨Large Slides

Displays the filmstrip with large slides so that you can see what is really on the slides. The difference between the views is shown in the figures in "Just the facts."

Just the facts

Selecting View Large Slides changes the overview of your slide show so that, on a standard VGA display, you have two rows of slides, with each row having three slides across. The slides are actually big enough to see.

When you work with a slide show, you are shown what I refer to as the *filmstrip view*. Within the filmstrip view, each slide is shown in its position within the slide show (reading from left to right and then top to bottom). This view lets you have an overall view of the organization of the presentation, but there are two things you have to balance — the number of slides you can see and the size of the slides. Large slides make it easy to see what is on each slide, but even with the window maximized on a standard VGA screen, you can see only six slides at a time.

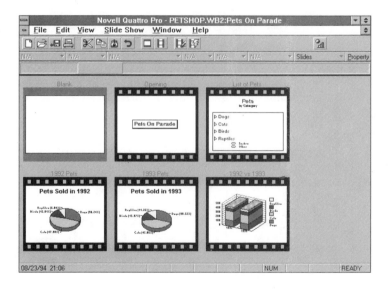

At the other extreme, you can view the small slides, which gives you a more complete overview of your slide show by showing more slides at one time (36 on a standard VGA display), but the slides are too small to make out any detail.

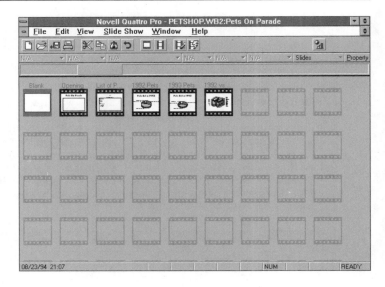

Of course, Goldilocks (and most political candidates) would take the compromise position and use medium slides. You can see 18 slides on a standard VGA screen with this view, and while you still can't see detail, you can at least tell the slides apart.

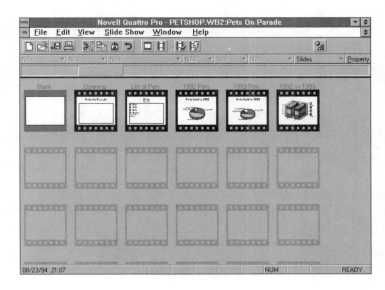

Which view you use is a matter of personal preference, and you can change between the three views very easily. There is, in fact a fourth choice on the View menu called Names Only, which doesn't show you the filmstrip view, but it gives you a list of the slides' names instead.

More stuff

How many slides you actually see in each view depends upon the resolution of your screen. The numbers listed are for a standard VGA 640 x 480 display. With a higher resolution, you would see more slides in each view.

 You can open any slide for editing by double-clicking on it. You can change the order of the slides in the presentation by dragging a slide to a new position. To change the transitions within the slide show, use the commands under Slide Show⇨Insert Slide.

 The other commands for getting an overview of your slide show are View⇨Medium Slides, View⇨Small Slides, and View⇨Name Only. To have a single slide displayed full-screen, use Slide Show⇨View Slide.

View⇨Locked Titles

Anchors the titles contained in the far left columns or the upper rows (or both) so that they stay on-screen while you scroll through the rest of the page. These titles make it easier for you to figure out what the numbers buried in the middle of the page refer to.

Just the facts

Selecting View⇨Locked Titles gives you a dialog box where you can freeze the rows that contain titles above the current cell, freeze the columns that contain titles to the left of the current cell, freeze both, or "unfreeze" any locked titles. A row or column is frozen when it is affected no longer by the scroll bar. (The term *locked titles* refers to either a set of frozen rows or a set of frozen columns or a combination of the two.)

If you select Horizontal from the Locked Titles dialog box, the rows above the current cell are frozen and do not move when you use the vertical scroll bar to view different rows. If you select Vertical from the dialog box, the columns to the left of the current cell are frozen. Selecting Both freezes both the rows above the cell and the columns to the left. Although you can freeze as many rows or columns as you wish, normally only the titles in the first few rows or the first few columns are frozen. Select the Clear option to "unfreeze" the locked titles.

More stuff

To have a row or column repeat as a heading on the printed page, use File⇨Print. To split your window so that you can look at two different parts of the notebook and scroll independently in each section, use View⇨Panes.

View⇨Medium Slides

Displays the slides on the filmstrip by using the compromise choice — large enough to give you a clue as to what is on the slide, but small enough so that you can see several slides at once.

Just the facts

With a standard VGA display, selecting View⇨Medium Slides displays the slide show overview with three rows of six slides each. With other screen resolutions the actual number will vary, but it will be more than with View⇨Large Slides and fewer than View⇨Small Slides. To see your other choices, check out the figures under View⇨Large Slides.

More stuff

You can open any slide for editing by double-clicking on it. You can change the order of the slides in the presentation by dragging a slide to a new position. To change the transitions within the slide show, use the commands under Slide Show⇨Insert Slide.

The other commands for controlling the look of the slide show overview are View⇨Large Slides, View⇨Small Slides and View⇨Name Only. To have a single slide displayed full-screen, use Slide Show⇨View Slide.

View⇨Name Only

Shows a list of the names of the slides in your slide show. This option is great only if you bothered to give your slides meaningful names.

Just the facts

View⇨Name Only changes the slide show overview into a list of the names of the slides in the presentation. Each slide is numbered and shown with an icon representing the type of slide. You can click on any slide and drag it to a new position or double-click on a slide to edit it.

More stuff

To have a single slide displayed full-screen, use Slide Show⇨View Slide. To see representations of the overall slide show with actual slide images, use View⇨Large Slides, View⇨Medium Slides, or View⇨Small Slides.

View⇨Objects Page

Takes you to the Objects Page, which is where things like graphs and slide shows are stored.

For mouse maniacs

⊠

When the SpeedTab points to the right, clicking it takes you to the Objects Page. (If it points to the left, you're already on the Objects Page and clicking it takes you to the notebook pages.)

Just the facts

When you select View⇨Objects Page, you jump immediately to the Objects Page. There's no waiting in line and no security check. The Objects Page displays an icon for each object (graph, slide show, dialog box, and so on) within your notebook. Even objects that have been created directly on the page (such as a graph) also have an icon on the Objects Page. You can double-click any object to edit it.

The SpeedTab button changes directions so that you can use it to get back to the current page in your notebook.

More stuff

The various objects in a notebook are each represented by a different icon. In fact, most of the different graph types have their own icons. Learning to recognize the icons saves you time because you can ignore all the objects that are the wrong type, and you don't have to keep opening a graph to figure out whether it's the one you want.

You can change the name of any graph by clicking on it once with the right mouse button and selecting Icon Properties (the first item on the pop-up menu). Now you are in the Name dialog box and can enter a new, more meaningful name. And, yes, you can use spaces. To change the name of a slide show, you follow the same basic steps, but the pop-up menu has a submenu with your choices on it (rather than a dialog box). Again, select the name and enter something you'll remember next time.

 To go back to the notebook page you came from, use View⇨Spreadsheet. To go to a particular location, use Edit⇨Go to.

View⇨Panes

Splits the current screen into smaller panes so that you can see different parts of the page at the same time. You can split the page either vertically or horizontally.

For mouse maniacs

 Drag the panes marker upward to split the screen into two horizontal panes or to the left to split the screen into two vertical panes.

Just the facts

If you want to split your window into two sections, you should first move to the spot where you want the division. You can then select View⇨Panes to display a dialog box with three options — Horizontal, Vertical, and Clear — and one check box (for Synchronize). If you move to the middle of your window and then go through the steps and pick the Horizontal option, you get a screen similar to the one in the figure.

Notice that each half of the screen has its own set of scroll bars and page tabs. If you choose the Synchronize option, using the horizontal scroll bars in either of the panes causes the contents of both panes to move together. With a synchronized horizontal split, you are always viewing the same columns. You can change the rows and pages shown in each pane independently.

If you select the Vertical option, the split runs up and down your screen, and the two sets of page tab markers and horizontal scroll bars are side by side. With a synchronized vertical split, you are always viewing the same row, and using either vertical scroll bar changes both panes. You can change the columns and pages independently.

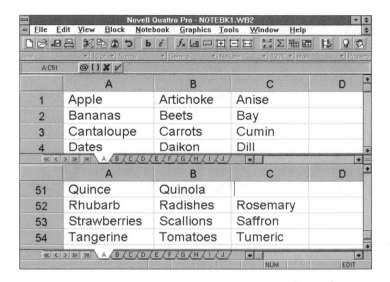

If you clear the Synchronize check box, you can change the columns, rows, and pages independently in each pane. You can clear the check box at any time.

To convert from splitting the panes in one direction to splitting in the other direction, you must first get rid of your original split. In the Panes dialog box, simply select the Clear option and then select OK.

More stuff

Using the pane indicator (in the lower-right corner of the window) to split the window is fairly easy. Place the cursor over the panes marker and hold it there until the cursor turns into the *split pane cursor* (a heavy black line with arrows out each side). If the line of the cursor is running horizontally, you can create a synchronized horizontal split. If the line is running vertically, you can create a synchronized vertical split. To change which cursor is displayed when you are creating a new pane, move the cursor toward a different edge of the pane indicator (the top for a horizontal split and the left side for a vertical split). To actually create the split, click on the panes marker and hold down the left mouse button while you drag the resulting dotted line to where you want the split.

To change the position of a split, drag the panes marker to a new location. To get rid of a split with a mouse, drag the panes marker back to the lower-right corner.

For another way of looking at your data, see Chapter 15 in *Quattro Pro 6 For Windows For Dummies*.

To have a separate window showing the notebook, use Window⟹New View. If you want to freeze a group of rows or columns so that they don't move when you scroll the rest of the notebook page, use View⟹Locked Titles.

View⟹Printer Preview

Shows the way your graph will be formatted on the page when you try to print it.

Just the facts

All you can do with View⟹Printer Preview is select it and look at the screen. What you see is a preview of what your graph will look like if you print it with the current settings. When you adjust the size of the window, the graph is shown at the largest possible size that maintains the proportions.

More stuff

For a more accurate rendering of your output and for access to the tools for making changes to the rest of the page, use the File⟹Print Preview command.

For a full screen graphic, use Graphics⟹View Graph. For other sample views, use View⟹35mm Slide, View⟹Floating Graph, View⟹Full Extent, or View⟹Screen Slide.

View⟹Screen Slide

Formats the graph with the proportions it would have if you used it as a slide in a slide show.

Just the facts

All you can do with View⟹Screen Slide is select it and look at the screen. The graph now has the same proportions as it will have if you run the slide show on your monitor. When you adjust the size of the window, the graph is shown at the largest possible size that maintains the proportions.

More stuff

For other sample views, you can use View⟹35mm Slide, View⟹Floating Graph, View⟹Full Extent, or View⟹Printer Preview. For a full screen graphic, use Graphics⟹View Graph.

View⟹Small Slides

Uses the smallest slide size for the filmstrip — which means you can see more slides at one time. The various sizes for the filmstrip are shown under "Just the facts" for the View⟹Large Slides command.

Just the facts

Selecting View⟹Small Slides gives the broadest overview of your slide show — showing you four rows, each with nine slides on a standard VGA display. You can tell what is on the slides — but only if you helped create them. To compare the three options for viewing the slide show filmstrip, see the figures under View⟹Large Slides.

More stuff

You can open any slide for editing by double-clicking on it. You can change the order of the slides in the presentation by dragging a slide to a new position. To change the transitions within the slide show, use the commands under Slide Show⟹Insert Slide.

You can change the filmstrip views by using View⟹Large Slides or View⟹Medium Slides. The alternative is to use View⟹Name Only. To have a single slide displayed full-screen, use Slide Show⟹View Slide.

View⟹Spreadsheet

Takes you back to the notebook page you were using before you went to the Objects Page.

For mouse maniacs

When the SpeedTab points to the left, clicking it jumps you to back to a notebook page. (If it points to the right, you're already on a notebook page and clicking it takes you to the Objects Page.)

Just the facts

The only use for the View⇨Spreadsheet command is to get back into your notebook pages from the Objects Page. Select the command, and you are returned to the current page.

More stuff

The buttons along the bottom of the window (covered under Edit⇨Go to) can be used to change the current page whether you are in the notebook or on the Objects Page.

To go to a particular location, use Edit⇨Go to. To jump to the Objects Page, use View⇨Objects Page.

View⇨*Zoom*

Controls the *zoom factor*, which is basically how much magnification the program uses to show you the notebook page. This is the feature with the most commands that do the same thing.

For mouse maniacs

The Zoom Factor list on the Property Band does the same thing as the View⇨Zoom command.

The Zoom To Fit button on the Modeling SpeedBar adjusts the zoom factor so that all the entries in the current table (a block surrounded by empty cells) are displayed in the highest possible magnification (the largest zoom factor).

Just the facts

Go to the View menu and select Zoom to see the Zoom Factor dialog box, with a less-than-exciting list of the possible zoom factors. Choose one and then choose whether it applies to the Page or the entire Notebook. After you select OK, your screen adjusts according to your wishes. A zoom factor of 100% is supposed to match the size of what you get from your printer. That's all there is to it.

More stuff

I think the most useful zoom factor option is Selection. When you highlight a block and then choose Selection, the selected block is sized to fill up the entire work area.

View⇨Zoom is the same setting as Active Page⇨Zoom Factor. To set the default zoom factor for the entire notebook, use Active Notebook⇨Zoom Factor.

Window ⇨ *Arrange Icons*

Arranges icons representing the various opened objects along the bottom of the screen. Each icon represents a separate object (such as a notebook view, graph, or slide show).

For mouse maniacs

The document's Minimize button appears on the document title bar if the document is in its own window or on the menu bar if the document window is maximized.

Just the facts

As soon as you select the <u>W</u>indow⇨<u>A</u>rrange Icons command, any windows that have been reduced to icons line up neatly in a row at the bottom.

To reduce a window to an icon, click on the Minimize button in the upper-left corner. If you click on the program's Minimize button by mistake, the entire program shrinks down to an icon on the Window desktop. Just double-click the icon to make it return to being a window.

Go to the <u>W</u>indow⇨<u>T</u>ile command to see an example of a set of arranged icons in the figure there.

More stuff

Each object within Quattro Pro is represented by a different icon. Learning to recognize the various icons makes it easier to find the item you are looking for when you are working with the Objects Page or with icons in the Quattro Pro window.

To arrange the windows, use either <u>W</u>indow⇨<u>C</u>ascade or <u>W</u>indow⇨<u>T</u>ile.

Window ⇨ *Cascade*

Organizes all the open windows so that each title bar is displayed. Because a picture is worth a thousand words, see "Just the facts" for an idea of what the cascade looks like. (I wish my publisher paid me the equivalent of a thousand words for one lousy picture.)

Just the facts

As soon as you select the <u>W</u>indow⇨<u>C</u>ascade command, your windows are rearranged (as shown in the accompanying figure).

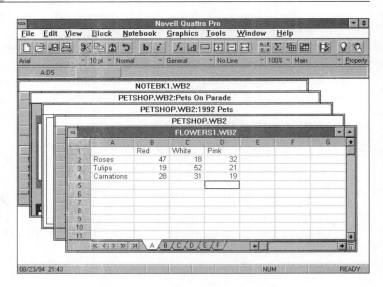

These windows are organized in a cascading fashion. No matter which one I pick, a little bit of each window will still be showing. Just click on the visible part of the window to make it active and move it to the top of the pile.

More stuff

For a window arrangement that lets you see each window, use Window⇨Tile.

Window⇨Hide

Removes the current window from the list on the Window menu and makes the window disappear. The notebook remains open and can be referenced from other notebooks. The window can contain the notebook or any object. This command is most useful when you are designing a system for someone else to use, and you don't want them to know how you designed the system.

Just the facts

Go to the window you want hidden and select Window⇨Hide. The current window seems to disappear. The information from the window is still available (and, in fact, can be used by other notebooks), but you can't see the window. This feature helps keep your work area less cluttered.

More stuff

If you hide a notebook and then try to open that notebook file, nothing happens. The only way to bring back a window is by using Window⇨Show.

To bring back a window, use Window⇨Show. You can hide part of a notebook by using Active Block⇨Reveal/Hide. For information on requiring a password to show a window, see Active Notebook⇨Password Level.

Window⇨List of Windows

Appears at the bottom of the Window menu as a numbered list and lets you quickly move between all the open windows. Each window can contain a notebook page, a graph, or a slide show. If part of a window is visible, you can just click directly on it.

Just the facts

To move to one of the objects on the list, simply select the object's name from the menu. This feature is most useful when you have maximized your windows and can, therefore, see only one window at a time. Otherwise, if part of the window that you want to work with is showing, you can just click on that part of the window to make it active and move it to the front.

More stuff

Windows that have been hidden with the Window⇨Hide command do not show up on the list of windows.

To arrange the various windows, use Window⇨Tile or Window⇨Cascade.

Window⇨New View

Opens a new window containing the current notebook. This command is particularly useful for when you want to compare the entries on two different pages with more flexibility than you can get with View⇨Panes.

Just the facts

Select Window⇨New View to open a new window containing the same notebook as the current window. Each window is identified by the window name followed by the window number. The second window displaying MYBOOK.WB2 would be titled MYBOOK.WB2:2. You can open as many different windows as you want.

More stuff

You can create a new view of a page by dragging the page tab onto the window background. Be careful not to release the mouse button while you are dragging the tab over the other tabs, or you'll end up moving the page instead of viewing it.

When you have several windows with the same notebook open, closing any single window does not close the notebook. Instead, the window with that view is closed, and the remaining windows are renumbered. When you have only one open window containing the notebook, closing that window then closes the notebook.

For another way of looking at your data, see Chapter 15 in *Quattro Pro 6 For Windows For Dummies*.

To split a single window, use View⇨Panes.

Window⇨Show

Displays a list of all hidden windows. If this command is available, the current database has at least one hidden window.

Just the facts

Selecting Window⇨Show gives you a list of all hidden windows. (If this command is not available, you don't have any windows that are not showing. In other words, all the windows are listed on the Window menu.) You can select only a single window at a time. To bring the window back, either double-click on the window name or click once and then click on the OK button. To bring back a second window, you need to select Window⇨Show again and go through the same steps.

More stuff

If a notebook has been deliberately hidden and protected using Active Notebook⇨Password Level, you have to provide the proper password in order to show the window. Notebooks are often hidden with this command because they contain macros that you are using as commands in your other notebooks. The window needs to be opened to make the macros available, but the person who created the macros doesn't want you changing them.

Hide your windows by using Window⇨Hide.

Window⇨Tile

Organizes all the open windows so that you can see the contents of each window. You don't necessarily see very much of the contents, but at least some of the window is showing.

Just the facts

Select this command to arrange the windows into separate tiles on-screen. The number of windows open determines the arrangement. The figure shows three windows that have been arranged with the Window⇨Tile command:

If any windows have been reduced to icons at the bottom of the screen, the tiling allows room to view the icons (as you can see in the figure). If no windows have been reduced to icons, the entire screen is used and there is no space at the bottom for icons.

More stuff

To view the windows by stacking them on top of each other, use the Window⇨Cascade command.

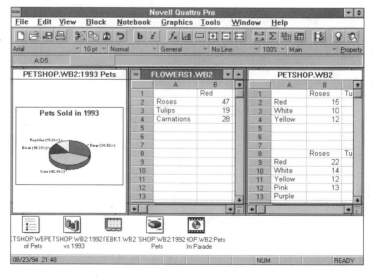

Part II

The Toolbar Tour

The Toolbar Tour

Because Quattro Pro uses the terms *toolbar* and *SpeedBar* interchangeably, I thought about calling this chapter the "SpeedBar Survey" but decided to be consistent with the other books. Besides, this tour covers not only the buttons in the toolbars but also the lists in the Property Band.

One of the main reasons for using a *For Dummies Quick Reference* is to learn faster and easier ways to use a program. (That's why it's called a Quick Reference.) In Quattro Pro, two types of shortcuts are worth learning. The first shortcut is the SpeedMenu: the pop-up menu that appears when you click the right mouse button. Commands that are in the SpeedMenus are marked with an icon (like the one to the left of this paragraph) throughout the rest of the book.

The second shortcut is using the left mouse button to select items from the SpeedBars or Property Bands. That's what this section is all about.

This Toolbar Tour presents each toolbar in its entirety, as well as each button in the toolbar. For each button, you get the button's name, a brief description of what the button does, and the menu command associated with the button (where you can look in the Command Reference for more information). It also shows the two main Property Bands (the Property Band and the Slide Property Band) and the lists in each.

You can have Quattro Pro display a button's or list's name by placing the mouse on the item. To activate this feature, which is called Balloon Hints, choose Application➪Display. Along with the Balloon Hint, Quattro Pro displays its description of the item in the title bar. You can get a slightly longer description by holding down the Ctrl key and right-clicking on the button or list.

Align SpeedBar

The Align Toolbar is used to position objects within the graph window. Many of the commands require you to have selected more than one object. The commands are intended for use with drawn objects rather than parts of the graph itself.

New Notebook: Gives you a new blank notebook for your creating pleasure (File➪New).

Open Notebook: Opens an existing notebook for use (File➪Open).

Save Notebook: Saves the current notebook, allowing you to name the notebook if it has not been saved previously (File⇨Save).

Print: Displays the Print dialog box, which enables you to format and print parts of your notebook (File⇨Print).

Cut: Removes the selected text or object and places it in the Clipboard (Edit⇨Cut).

Copy: Copies the selected text or object to the Clipboard (Edit⇨Copy).

Paste: Inserts whatever is in the Clipboard (Edit⇨Paste).

Undo/Redo: Reverses the last action, even if the last action was an Undo (Edit⇨Undo).

Align Left: Arranges the selected objects so that the handles along their left sides are aligned (Tools⇨Align).

Align Right: Arranges the selected objects so that the handles along their right sides are aligned (Tools⇨Align).

Align Top: Arranges the selected objects so that their top handles are aligned (Tools⇨Align).

Align Bottom: Arranges the selected objects so that their bottom handles are aligned (Tools⇨Align).

Vertical Center: Arranges the selected objects so that their centers fall along a line that runs left to right through the center of the graph (Tools⇨Align).

Horizontal Center: Arranges the selected objects so that their centers fall along a line that runs top to bottom through the center of the graph (Tools⇨Align).

Horizontal Space: Positions the selected objects the specified distance from one another across the graph, from left to right (Tools⇨Align).

Vertical Space: Positions the selected objects the specified distance from one another across the graph, from top to bottom (Tools⇨Align).

Bring Forward: Moves the selected object one layer closer to the viewer (Tools⇨Object Order).

Send Backward: Moves the selected object one layer away from the viewer (Tools⇨Object Order).

Bring to Front: Makes the selected object the closest one to the viewer (Tools⇨Object Order).

Send to Back: Makes the selected object the farthest one from the viewer (Tools⇨Object Order).

Group: Combines the selected objects into a single object for moving and resizing (Tools⇨Group).

Ungroup: Breaks the grouped object into individual objects (Tools⇨Ungroup).

Block SpeedBar

The Block Toolbar is available when you're working with the notebook page. This toolbar contains a variety of buttons that are useful for working with blocks of cells.

New Notebook: Gives you a new blank notebook for your creating pleasure (File⇨New).

Open Notebook: Opens an existing notebook for use (File⇨Open).

Save Notebook: Saves the current notebook, allowing you to name the notebook if it has not been saved previously (File⇨Save).

Print: Displays the Print dialog box, which enables you to format and print parts of your notebook (File⇨Print).

Cut: Removes the selected text or object and places it in the Clipboard (Edit⇨Cut).

Copy: Copies the selected text or object to the Clipboard (Edit⇨Copy).

Paste: Inserts whatever is in the Clipboard (Edit⇨Paste).

Paste Link: Inserts the contents of the Clipboard and creates a link to the source (Edit⇨Paste Special).

Undo/Redo: Reverses the last action, even if the last action was an Undo (Edit⇨Undo).

Clear: Removes everything, including formatting, from the cells (Edit⇨Clear).

Clear Values: Removes the contents of cells but leaves any formatting or properties intact (Edit⇨Clear Values).

Transpose: Switches the contents of the rows and columns within the block (Block⇨Transpose).

Values: Replaces any formulas in the block with their values (Block⇨Values).

⊞ **Insert:** Inserts a row or column if one is selected, or displays the Block Insert dialog box (Block⇨Insert).

⊟ **Delete:** Removes a row or column if one is selected, or displays the Block Delete dialog box (Block⇨Delete).

▥ **SpeedSort (Ascending Sort):** Sorts the selected block in ascending order, based on the values in the first column (Block⇨Sort).

▥ **SpeedSort (Descending Sort):** Sorts the selected block in descending order, based on the values in the first column (Block⇨Sort).

Σ **SpeedSum:** Inserts an @Sum() function along the bottom or to the right to add the cells in the block (SpeedSum).

▦ **SpeedFill:** Fills the selected block with a series of numbers or labels (SpeedFill).

▦ **Model Copy:** Opens the Block Copy dialog box so that you can copy the selected block (Block⇨Copy).

🔲 **Experts:** Provides a dialog box for starting any of the eight Quattro Pro Experts (Help⇨Experts).

🔲 **Coaches:** Lets you start one of the Quattro Pro Coaches, which helps you complete common tasks (Help⇨Coaches).

Draw SpeedBar

The Draw Toolbar, which is one of the toolbars available for work with notebook pages, allows you to add various types of objects to your page. For information on using the drawing tools (Line through Text), see the section on the Graph Toolbar.

🔲 **New Notebook:** Gives you a new blank notebook for your creating pleasure (File⇨New).

🔲 **Open Notebook:** Opens an existing notebook for use (File⇨Open).

🔲 **Save Notebook:** Saves the current notebook, allowing you to name the notebook if it has not been saved previously (File⇨Save).

🔲 **Print:** Displays the Print dialog box, which enables you to format and print parts of your notebook (File⇨Print).

🔲 **Cut:** Removes the selected text or object and places it in the Clipboard (Edit⇨Cut).

Copy: Copies the selected text or object to the Clipboard (Edit⇨Copy).

Paste: Inserts whatever is in the Clipboard (Edit⇨Paste).

Undo/Redo: Reverses the last action, even if the last action was an Undo (Edit⇨Undo).

Graph Tool: Enables you to draw a graph on the page, using the selected block of cells (Graphics⇨New Graph).

SpeedButton Tool: Creates a button object that you can use to activate a macro. (The command is not covered in this reference; it's just too complex.)

Line Tool: Draws a line as an object on the page (see the Graph Toolbar section).

Arrow Tool: Draws a line with an arrowhead as an object on the page (see the Graph Toolbar section).

Rectangle Tool: Draws a regular rectangle or square as an object on the page (see the Graph Toolbar section).

Rounded Rectangle Tool: Draws a rectangle or square with rounded corners as an object on the page (see the Graph Toolbar section).

Ellipse Tool: Draws an oval or circle as an object on the page (see the Graph Toolbar section).

Text Tool: Creates a box containing your text as an object on the page (see the Graph Toolbar section).

Lasso Tool: Draws a dashed-line rectangle that you can use to surround and select objects. To use the Lasso, click on the Lasso Tool button, move to a position above and to the left of the objects, hold down the mouse button, and drag downward and to the right. A dashed-line rectangle surrounds the objects. When you release the mouse button, the objects inside the rectangle should be selected.

Insert Object: Enables you to use an object created by another program (Edit⇨Insert Object).

Bring Forward: Moves the selected object one layer closer to the viewer (Tools⇨Object Order).

Send Backward: Moves the selected object one layer away from the viewer (Tools⇨Object Order).

Bring to Front: Makes the selected object the closest one to the viewer (Tools⇨Object Order).

Send to Back: Makes the selected object the farthest one from the viewer (Tools⇨Object Order).

Experts: Provides a dialog box for starting any of the eight Quattro Pro Experts (Help⇨Experts).

Coaches: Lets you start one of the Quattro Pro Coaches, which helps you complete common tasks (Help⇨Coaches).

Format SpeedBar

You use the Format Toolbar to format blocks on your notebook page. Most of its commands set block properties which are discussed in the command reference under the entries for Active Block.

New Notebook: Gives you a new blank notebook for your creating pleasure (File⇨New).

Open Notebook: Opens an existing notebook for use (File⇨Open).

Save Notebook: Saves the current notebook, allowing you to name the notebook if it has not been saved previously (File⇨Save).

Print: Displays the Print dialog box, which enables you to format and print parts of your notebook (File⇨Print).

Cut: Removes the selected text or object and places it in the Clipboard (Edit⇨Cut).

Copy: Copies the selected text or object to the Clipboard (Edit⇨Copy).

Paste: Inserts whatever is in the Clipboard (Edit⇨Paste).

Paste Properties: Sets the properties of the selected block of cells to match those of the block in the Clipboard (Edit⇨Paste Special).

Undo/Redo: Reverses the last action, even if the last action was an Undo (Edit⇨Undo).

Bold: Makes the text in the selected block bold (Active Block⇨Font).

Italic: Makes the text in the selected block italic (Active Block⇨Font).

Underline: Underlines the text in the selected block (Active Block⇨Font).

Font Size Arrows: Increases (up arrow) or decreases (down arrow) the font size (Active Block⇨Font).

Word Wrap: Causes the text within a cell to wrap to more than one line (Active Block⇨Alignment).

Orientation: Formats the text to be read from top to bottom rather than left to right (Active Block⇨Alignment).

Vertical Alignment: Bottom: Places the text flush with the bottom edge of the cell (Active Block⇨Alignment).

Vertical Alignment: Center: Centers the text between the top and bottom edges of the cell (Active Block⇨Alignment).

Vertical Align: Top: Places the text flush with the top edge of the cell (Active Block⇨Alignment).

Line Draw: Opens a dialog box that enables you to place borders around a block (Active Block⇨Line Drawing).

SpeedFormat: Opens a dialog box in which you can choose a format for the block (SpeedFormat).

Shading: Opens a dialog box in which you can choose the background shading for the block (Active Block⇨Shading).

Text Color: Opens a dialog box in which you can set the color of the text within the block (Active Block⇨Text Color).

Experts: Provides a dialog box for starting any of the eight Quattro Pro Experts (Help⇨Experts).

Coaches: Lets you start one of the Quattro Pro Coaches, which helps you complete common tasks (Help⇨Coaches).

Graph SpeedBar

The Graph Toolbar contains a variety of tools for creating objects as part of a graph. Most of these tools do not exist as menu commands and can be used only with the mouse. That's why this chapter is the only place in this book where these tools are explained.

When you use the drawing tools, the cursor changes to a plus sign with an attached outline of the button to remind you what you intend to draw. Some of these tools are duplicated in the Draw Toolbar, where they are used to create objects that float above the notebook page.

New Notebook: Gives you a new blank notebook for your creating pleasure (File⇨New).

Open Notebook: Opens an existing notebook for use (File⇨Open).

Save Notebook: Saves the current notebook, allowing you to name the notebook if it has not been saved previously (File⇨Save).

Print: Displays the Print dialog box, which enables you to format and print parts of your notebook (File➪Print).

Cut: Removes the selected text or object and places it in the Clipboard (Edit➪Cut).

Copy: Copies the selected text or object to the Clipboard (Edit➪Copy).

Paste: Inserts whatever is in the Clipboard (Edit➪Paste).

Undo/Redo: Reverses the last action, even if the last action was an Undo (Edit➪Undo).

Import: Opens a dialog box for importing graphic images created in other programs (Tools➪Import Graphics).

Selection Tool: Selects one or more objects. You can click on a single object to select it. You can also hold down the Shift key and click on an object to add it to a group. If an object is already in a group, you can hold down the Shift key and click on it to remove it from the group.

You can use this tool to create a selection marquee (or rectangle), as you can with the Lasso Tool in the Draw Toolbar. To use the selection marquee, click on the button, move to a position above and to the left of the objects you want to select, hold down the mouse button, and drag down and to the right of the objects. A dashed-line rectangle surrounds the objects. When you release the mouse button, the objects in the rectangle are selected.

The following three commands are used to draw straight lines on the graph.

Line Tool: Draws a straight line. Move the mouse to where you want the line to start, click the left mouse button, and drag to where the line should end. Right-click on the line to change the color and style of the line.

Arrow Tool: Draws a straight line with an arrowhead at the end. Move the mouse to where you want the line to start, click the left mouse button, and drag to where the line should end. The arrowhead appears at this end of the line. Right-click on the line to change the two colors and shading pattern (Style) used for the arrowhead, as well as the color and style of the line.

Polyline Tool: Draws a series of connected straight lines. Move the mouse to where you want the line to start, and click the left mouse button. Each additional click connects the current point and the preceding point with a straight line. Double-click to stop drawing. Right-click on the line to change the color and style of the line.

Freehand Polyline Tool: Draws a freehand line. Move the mouse to where you want the line to start, click the left mouse button, and drag to draw a line as the mouse's trail. The line that you draw follows the movements of the mouse and is not restricted to being a straight line. Release the mouse button to stop drawing. Right-click on the line to change the color and style of the line.

Text Tool: Creates a rectangle to contain text. Move to the upper-left corner of where you want the text to appear, click the mouse button, and drag to the lower-left corner. To insert the text, click inside the rectangle and start typing. Right-click anywhere within the box to change the color and style of the text or of the box. Both the text and box use two colors and a shading pattern (called Style by Quattro Pro). You can also change the alignment of the text, as well as the color and style of the border.

Each of the following five tools creates a closed shape. You can right-click to change the two colors and the shading pattern (Style) within the object, as well as the color and style of the border.

Polygon Tool: Draws a closed figure of straight lines. The Polygon Tool works very much like the Polyline Tool, except that when you double-click, Quattro Pro draws a line from the last point to the first. Move to where you want to start drawing, and click one time. Move to the next point to be connected with a straight line, and click again. Continue this procedure until you reach the last new point; then double-click to connect the last point with the first.

Rectangle Tool: Draws a regular rectangle or a square. Move to where you want the upper-left corner of the rectangle to be, and drag to where you want the lower-right corner to be. If you hold down the Shift key while dragging, you draw a square.

Rounded Rectangle Tool: Draws a rectangle or square with rounded corners. Just as you do with the regular Rectangle Tool, move to where you want the upper-left corner of the rectangle to be, and drag to where you want the lower-right corner to be. If you hold down the Shift key while dragging, you draw a square with rounded corners.

Ellipse Tool: Draws an oval or a circle. Imagine that there is a rectangle around the oval that you want to draw, and move to the upper-left corner of that imaginary rectangle. Hold down the mouse button and drag to the lower right. If you hold down the Shift key while dragging, you draw a circle.

Freehand Polygon Tool: Allows you to draw a freehand line and then draws a straight line to close the figure. Hold down the mouse button and drag to create the line. The line follows any movements of the mouse. When you finish drawing, release the mouse button; Quattro Pro draws a straight line to close the figure.

Block Tool: Allows you to create a rectangle that contains a portion of a notebook page. Move to where you want the upper-corner of the block to be, hold down the mouse button, and drag to the lower-right corner of the block. When you release the mouse button, Quattro Pro displays a dialog box that enables you to select the block to display and to specify whether to show the borders (the column letters and row numbers), the grid lines (the lines between the rows and columns), both, or neither. Choose Maintain Aspect Ratio so that any resizing of the block does not distort the shape of the cells.

Graph Gallery: Opens a dialog box in which you can choose a style for the selected graph (Graphics⇨Graph Gallery).

Main SpeedBar

This is the toolbar that Quattro Pro displays automatically when you work with a notebook page. The Main Toolbar contains the buttons that the designers of Quattro Pro thought would be the most useful.

New Notebook: Gives you a new blank notebook for your creating pleasure (File⇨New).

Open Notebook: Opens an existing notebook for use (File⇨Open).

Save Notebook: Saves the current notebook, allowing you to name the notebook if it has not been saved previously (File⇨Save).

Print: Displays the Print dialog box, which enables you to format and print parts of your notebook (File⇨Print).

Cut: Removes the selected text or object and places it in the Clipboard (Edit⇨Cut).

Copy: Copies the selected text or object to the Clipboard (Edit⇨Copy).

Paste: Inserts whatever is in the Clipboard (Edit⇨Paste).

Undo/Redo: Reverses the last action, even if the last action was an Undo (Edit⇨Undo).

Bold: Makes the text in the selected block bold (Active Block⇨Font).

Italic: Makes the text in the selected block italic (Active Block⇨Font).

Formula Composer: Opens the Formula Composer, which helps you create a formula (Tools⇨Formula Composer).

Graph Tool: Allows you to draw a graph on the page, using the selected block of cells (Graphics⇨New Graph).

SpeedButton Tool: Creates a button object that you can use to activate a macro. (The command is not covered in this reference; it's just too complex.)

Insert: Inserts a row or column if one is selected, or displays the Block Insert dialog box (Block⇨Insert).

Delete: Removes a row or column if one is selected, or displays the Block Delete dialog box (Block⇨Delete).

Fit: Adjusts the width of the column to match the longest entry in the column (Active Block⇨Column Width).

SpeedSort (Ascending Sort): Sorts the selected block in ascending order, based on the values in the first column (Block⇨Sort).

SpeedSort (Descending Sort): Sorts the selected block in descending order, based on the values in the first column (Block⇨Sort).

SpeedSum: Inserts an @Sum() function along the bottom or to the right to add the cells in the block (SpeedSum).

SpeedFill: Fills the selected block with a series of numbers or labels (SpeedFill).

SpeedFormat: Opens a dialog box in which you can choose a format for the block (SpeedFormat).

Edit Slide Show: Opens a dialog box in which you can select a slide show to edit (Graphics⇨Edit Slide Show and Slide Show⇨Insert Slide).

Experts: Provides a dialog box for starting any of the eight Quattro Pro Experts (Help⇨Experts).

Coaches: Lets you start one of the Quattro Pro Coaches, which helps you complete common tasks (Help⇨Coaches).

Modeling SpeedBar

The Modeling Toolbar is the advanced toolbar. It contains buttons that are designed to work with the complex commands located in the Tools menus.

New Notebook: Gives you a new blank notebook for your creating pleasure (File⇨New).

Open Notebook: Opens an existing notebook for use (File⇨Open).

Save Notebook: Saves the current notebook, allowing you to name the notebook if it has not been saved previously (File⇨Save).

Print: Displays the Print dialog box, which enables you to format and print parts of your notebook (File⇨Print).

Cut: Removes the selected text or object and places it in the Clipboard (Edit⇨Cut).

Copy: Copies the selected text or object to the Clipboard (Edit⇨Copy).

Paste: Inserts whatever is in the Clipboard (Edit⇨Paste).

Undo/Redo: Reverses the last action, even if the last action was an Undo (Edit⇨Undo).

Open Links: Opens any notebooks that are referenced in the current notebook's formulas and updates those formulas (Notebook⇨Update Links).

Refresh Links: Updates any formulas in the current notebook that reference another notebook without opening the other notebook (Notebook⇨Update Links).

Select Entire Table: Starts with the current cell and selects the smallest possible block of cells with a row or column of empty cells along each side (Edit⇨Select All).

Top Left of Table: Jumps to the upper-left corner of the current table, which is bordered by a row and column of empty cells (Edit⇨Go To).

Top Right of Table: Jumps to the upper-right corner of the current table, which is bordered by a row and column of empty cells (Edit⇨Go To).

Bottom Left of Table: Jumps to the lower-left corner of the current table, which is bordered by a row and column of empty cells (Edit⇨Go To).

Bottom Right of Table: Jumps to the lower-right corner of the current table, which is bordered by a row and column of empty cells (Edit⇨Go To).

Zoom to Fit: Scales the current selection or table to fill the entire work area (View⇨Zoom).

Data Modeling Desktop: Opens the Data Modeling Desktop program (Tools⇨Data Modeling Desktop).

Database Desktop: Opens the Database Desktop program (Tools⇨Database Desktop).

Scenario Manager: Opens the Scenario Manager dialog box (Tools⇨Scenario Manager).

Consolidator: Opens the Consolidator dialog box, which enables you to consolidate blocks of cells (Tools⇨Consolidator).

Table Link: Opens a dialog box for creating a link to a database table (Tools⇨Database Tools).

Experts: Provides a dialog box for starting any of the eight Quattro Pro Experts (Help⇨Experts).

Coaches: Lets you start one of the Quattro Pro Coaches, which helps you complete common tasks (Help⇨Coaches).

Objects SpeedBar

The Objects Toolbar appears only on the Objects Page (View⇨Objects Page). This toolbar contains commands for creating new objects, as well as for working with existing objects (you can cut and copy entire objects and paste them in the current notebook or in another notebook). To edit an object, double-click on its icon.

New Notebook: Gives you a new blank notebook for your creating pleasure (File⇨New).

Open Notebook: Opens an existing notebook for use (File⇨Open).

Save Notebook: Saves the current notebook, allowing you to name the notebook if it has not been saved previously (File⇨Save).

Print: Displays the Print dialog box, which enables you to format and print parts of your notebook (File⇨Print).

Cut: Removes the selected text or object and places it in the Clipboard (Edit⇨Cut).

Copy: Copies the selected text or object to the Clipboard (Edit⇨Copy).

Paste: Inserts whatever is in the Clipboard (Edit⇨Paste).

Undo/Redo: Reverses the last action, even if the last action was an Undo (Edit⇨Undo).

New Graph: Creates a new graph by entering the series in the Graph New dialog box (Graphics⇨New Graph and Graphics⇨Series).

Create Slide Show: Allows you to name a new slide show and displays the filmstrip view, along with the Slides menu and the Slides Property Band (Graphics⇨New Slide Show).

New Dialog: Opens the tools for creating a dialog box (much too complex for this reference).

Run Slide Show: Provides a dialog box for selecting a slide show to run (Graphics➪Run Slide Show).

Coaches: Lets you start one of the Quattro Pro Coaches, which helps you complete common tasks (Help➪Coaches).

Palette SpeedBar

| Standard |⬇| ▪▪ ▪▪ ▪▪▪▪ ▪▪ ▪ | Color |

The Palette Toolbar, which is available when you work with a graph, is used to change the color and pattern of the interior of an object or group of objects in the graph. To change an object's interior, select the object and click on a choice in the palette. If you don't see what you want in the current palette, you can select a different color from the Palette List. The Color box shows the current interior for the object. The options for setting these features are not available in menu commands; to access them, right-click the object.

| Standard |⬇| **Palette List:** Use this list to select one of the predefined color palettes. You can select solid colors from most of the palettes, or you can use the special palettes for Blends (pairs of colors) or Washes (white to a solid color). Use the ColorPatterns palette to apply two-color patterns.

Print Preview SpeedBar

| Page |1| of 1 |🔼|🔽| Zoom: 100 % |🔍|🔍| 🎞 | ▢▢▢▢▢ | ✖ |

The Print Preview Toolbar appears, surprisingly enough, only after you choose the File➪Print Preview command. The Options button does not appear when you preview a graph.

| Page [1] of 1 | **Page Indicator:** Type the number of the page that you want to view, and press Enter to jump to that page (File➪Print Preview).

Previous Page: Moves to the preceding page (File➪Print Preview).

Next Page: Moves to the next page (File➪Print Preview).

Zoom In: Increases the magnification of the page to make the text bigger (File➪Print Preview).

Zoom Out: Decreases the magnification of the page to make the text smaller (File➪Print Preview).

Color: Changes from a color preview to a black-and-white preview (File➪Print Preview).

Margin: Opens the dialog box in which you can set the page's margins (File➪Page Setup).

Setup: Displays the Page Setup dialog box (File➪Page Setup).

🖵 **Options:** Displays the Spreadsheet Print Options dialog box (File⇨Print).

🖶 **Print:** Starts printing your document (File⇨Print).

❌ **Exit Preview:** Takes you out of Print Preview (File⇨Print Preview).

Property Band

| Arial | ▾ | 10 pt ▾ | Normal | ▾ | General | ▾ | No Line | ▾ | 100% ▾ | Main | ▾ | Property |

The standard Property Band is available whenever you work with a notebook page, and a very similar one is available when you work with graphs. The only time that the Property Band is really different is when you work with slides.

The items in the Property Band are lists rather than buttons. Click on the item one time to display the list, and then click on one of the list's entries to select it. If necessary, you can use the scroll bar to display more of the list. If you prefer, you can click the mouse button while the mouse is on the Property Band item and hold the button down while you drag down the list to select the item. To select the item, release the mouse button.

▭ Arial **Font:** Sets the font for the selected block (Active Block⇨Font).

▭ 10 pt **Font Size:** Sets the size of the font for the selected block (Active Block⇨Font).

▭ Normal **Style:** Sets the properties for the selected block, using the style's definition (Notebook⇨Define Styles). When you work with graphs, the list in this position is the Color Sets list, from which you can select a color scheme for your graph (Graphics⇨Edit Graph and Graphics⇨Graph Gallery).

▭ General **Align:** Sets the alignment for the contents of the cells in the selected block (Active Block⇨Alignment).

▭ No Line **Underline:** Sets the border for the bottom edge of the box (Active Block⇨Line Drawing).

▭ 100% **Zoom Factor:** Sets the magnification of the current page (Active Page⇨Zoom Factor).

▭ Main **Toolbars:** Specifies which toolbar is displayed (SpeedBars).

▭ Slides **Property:** Displays the Property dialog box for the item that you select from the list (Property⇨*Object*).

Slide Property Band

Use Master	No Overlay	Wipe right	Fast	0.5 min	Show Slide	Slides	Property

The Slide Property Band, which appears when you work with a slide show, contains the tools for setting the transitions between slides. None of these commands has a menu equivalent, but you can make choices in the Slides dialog box. To get to the Slides dialog box, position your cursor over a slide and click the right mouse button and then select Slide Properties from the menu that appears.

Use Master Slide: Specifies whether the master slide is used as the background for the current slide (Slide Show⇨Insert Slide).

Overlay Previous Slide: Specifies whether the preceding slide is left on-screen to be used as the background for the current slide (Slide Show⇨Insert Slide).

Effect: Sets the transition effect between the preceding slide and the current slide (Slide Show⇨Insert Slide).

Speed: Sets the speed of the transition between the preceding slide and the current slide (Slide Show⇨Insert Slide).

Display Time: Specifies how long the current slide is displayed. You can set this interval more precisely by using the Slide property dialog box (Slide Show⇨Insert Slide).

Show/Skip Slide: Specifies whether to show or skip the current slide (Slide Show⇨Insert Slide).

Toolbars: Specifies which toolbar is displayed (Slide Show⇨Insert Slide).

Property: Displays the Property dialog box for the item that you select from the list (Property⇨*Object*).

Slides SpeedBar

The Slides Toolbar, which appears when you edit a slide show, contains buttons that execute the basic slide-show commands.

New Notebook: Gives you a new blank notebook for your creating pleasure (File⇨New).

Open Notebook: Opens an existing notebook for use (File⇨Open).

Save Notebook: Saves the current notebook, allowing you to name the notebook if it has not been saved previously (File⇨Save).

Print: Displays the Print dialog box, which enables you to format and print parts of your notebook (File⇨Print).

Cut: Removes the selected text or object and places it in the Clipboard (Edit⇨Cut).

Copy: Copies the selected text or object to the Clipboard (Edit⇨Copy).

Paste: Inserts whatever is in the Clipboard (Edit⇨Paste).

Undo/Redo: Reverses the last action, even if the last action was an Undo (Edit⇨Undo).

New Graph: Creates a new graph by entering the series in the Graph New dialog box (Graphics⇨New Graph and Graphics⇨Series).

Create Slide Show: Allows you to name a new slide show and displays the filmstrip view, along with the Slides menu and the Slides Property Band (Graphics⇨New Slide Show).

Edit Slide Show: Opens a dialog box in which you can select a slide show to edit (Graphics⇨Edit Slide Show and Slide Show⇨Insert Slide).

Run Slide Show: Runs the selected slide show or displays a dialog box in which you can select a slide show to run (Graphics⇨Run Slide Show).

Graph Gallery: Opens a dialog box in which you can choose a style for the selected graph (Graphics⇨Graph Gallery).

Index

❏ YES!
Please keep me informed about IDG's World
of Computer Knowledge. Send me the latest
IDG Books catalog.

COMPUTER
BOOK SERIES
FROM IDG